The Woo Way

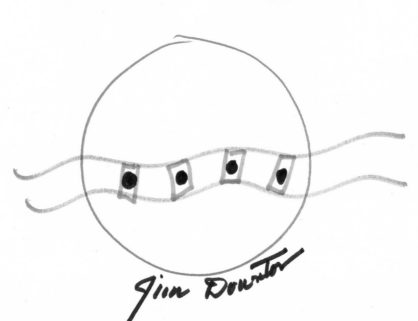

Jim Downton

The Woo Way

A New Way of Living and Being

James Downton, Jr.

Humanics Trade Group
Atlanta, GA USA

HUMANICS
The Woo Way
A Humanics Trade Group Publication

Humanics trade Group Publications are an imprint of and published by Humanics Publishing Group, a division of Brumby Holdings, Inc. Its trademark, consisting of the words "Humanics Trade Group" and a portrayal of a Pegasus, is registered in the U.S. Patent Office and in other countries.

Brumby Holdings, Inc.
1197 Peachtree St.
Suite 533B Plaza
Atlanta, GA 30361
USA

Printed in the United States of America and the United Kingdom

Library of Congress Control Number: 2001091309
ISBN (Paperback): 0-89334-349-8
ISBN (Hardcover): 0-89334-348-X

Dedication

For my students

Bright,
Courageous,
Creative,
Kind.

I will never forget you.

Woo Master:
"When old way is not working, new way opens."

Contents

Chapter 3: I Want To Look Good And Be Accepted 21

We try to look good and be accepted by others. When we succeed, we feel great. When we fail, we feel terrible. Awareness of this automatic pattern gives us the choice to embrace looking bad and rejection so we can care less about proving our worth to others.

Chapter 4: I Want Independence And Control 29

Independence and control are prized in our society. When we achieve them, confidence gives rise to good feelings and success. When we fail, we may feel trapped, dominated, and unhappy. Through awareness, a new way to deal with these issues is discovered.

Chapter 5: I Want To Be Right 35

Imagine someone saying to you, "You're wrong." How do you automatically react? Probably with resistance, because we love being right and dislike being wrong about our beliefs. Being right gives us a feeling of control and certainty. Knowing this, we get to make a change.

Chapter 6: I Need To Feel Safe 39

Human beings have many fears. Some are obvious and others dominate us from the shadows. We are constantly managing our safety so we can survive and succeed. When we know what controls us in the realm of security, new choices appear.

Chapter 7: Restoring A Shrinking Ego 45

Our egos are like balloons that constantly expand and deflate. We love the inflations, but suffer from the deflations. There is a way to restore the size of a shrinking ego by making a "recovery claim." When we do, we develop more control over our reactions to what others say or do.

Part II
Everyone Is Telling Stories

We may suffer because of the stories we tell ourselves and others. When we are aware of how our stories undermine our well-being and our relationships, we can put a stop to them. The next chapters uncover the different stories we tell and reveal the price we pay for telling them.

Two deceptive practices we employ in our storytelling are omission of the truth and giving false information, also known as blatant lying. These forms of deception can damage our relationships because they undermine trust. Honesty has the opposite effect.

Watch what people do, not just what they say. How many people say one thing and do another? Do we trust their word? When we honestly communicate what we intend to do, then do it, we begin to live with greater integrity. Others trust what we say, so our relationships work better.

Since our minds want certainty, we make up stories about people and situations where we have little or no information. We can suffer from the stories we make up. When we quit telling the stories and just state the facts, we put a stop to the suffering and move into greater effectiveness.

Do we blame something in the past for our lives not working? How many of us create stories about the present that limit us and make us unhappy? How many of us paint a bleak picture of the future? Understanding what we get from those stories, a new choice appears.

Part III
Making Relationships Work

Trying to make relationships work well is challenging. We may wonder why it is so difficult and how to make it easier. In the following chapters, new ways of thinking about relationships emerge, so new choices and practices appear.

lems or improving them when things are going well. A strategy for co-creating ideas to solve problems and improve relationships is introduced and practiced.

Chapter 19: Cleaning Up Relationships 145
Knowing how to clean up relationships is important. When we fail to do the clean up work, the past can become a heavy weight on our minds. Forgiveness, acceptance, and completion are ways of cleaning up our relationships, so the present and future become our focus.

Part IV
Developing Balance, Wholeness, And Wisdom

We live out of balance and pay a price. In the following chapters, we explore our dual nature, our tendency to suffer from negative thoughts, and how we can cultivate more balance, wholeness, and wisdom in our lives.

Chapter 20: Life Out Of Balance 155
We suffer from living in a one-sided way, because we are of two minds. We have a dual nature, so contradiction is not something to avoid but embrace. When we integrate the opposites within us, we become more balanced, which is a goal of "individuation."

Chapter 21: Shadow Projection 161
Wanting to look good, we project our neglected shadow side onto others, and then dislike or hate them for it. Awareness of this pattern gives us the opportunity to take back our projections and reclaim the two sides of our nature.

Chapter 22: Cultivating Wisdom 165
Instead of looking to others for wisdom, we seek wisdom from within ourselves. To cultivate it, we consult with our inner wise person and then discover that we already carry wisdom in our pocket. When we use it, our lives work better.

Many of us construct mental torture chambers where we suffer "on the rack" of our own negative thinking. Becoming aware of this pattern, we get into the "director's chair" and learn to stop the thoughts that make us suffer.

Worriers suffer from exaggerated estimates of bad things happening. By understanding fear as a thought that magnifies misfortune, we claim more freedom of choice about it. By using the "1% rule," the size of our fear is reduced so it no longer stops us automatically.

We expect and desire things to be a certain way and when they appear otherwise, we become frustrated or angry. By putting up resistance to the way life occurs, we cultivate stress and lives of discontent. By stopping the resistance, living becomes easier.

Some of us are experts at making little problems into big ones, then we suffer from the added weight. When we learn to see with the eyes of the mouse and the buffalo, we reduce the size of our problems. With less weighty problems, we have less weighty lives.

Our lives are our own creations. Using our creativity, we invent a new identity, life purposes, and ethnical principles as if our life were starting now. We make up the reasons why we were born in order to make our lives count.

Appreciation

I deeply appreciate and admire the many people who have done the work of *The Woo Way* with me, both at the University of Colorado (Boulder) and in the community. It was an honor to watch them deepen their awareness, make new choices, start new life practices, and work for change. Some have joined me in becoming apprentices of the inner Woo Master, that part of us which is already whole and wise. They are now part of this life gardening project.

There are influences that have made their mark on my thinking. I appreciate the ideas I absorbed from the EST training during the early 1970s and subsequent work with Landmark Education, a learning center which offers life-changing courses in major cities around the world. To discover what this educational organization offers, see its website:[www.landmarkeducation.com]. Also, I have been heavily influenced by the work of Carl G. Jung, the Swiss psychologist who gave us such a deep understanding of the nature of human beings and the process of becoming whole, which he called "individuation."

Special thanks to Marty Dick for helping me craft my writing to make it "wooish," not too wordy, but wordy enough. She was also the first person to lead a group using *The Woo Way*, which produced impressive results for those involved. Finally, I want to thank my wife, Mary, who helped me sharpen and simplify my writing style, while offering helpful suggestions about the work's design.

Finally, I want to acknowledge the people who help others improve their lives and who tend to the well-being of our planet. The projects they serve make a difference and give people hope for the future. Heifer International is one of those projects. A global organization, its purpose is to end hunger, so children and their families can lead healthier, happier, and more productive lives. Half of my royalties from *The Woo Way* will go to that worthwhile project. To learn more about its work, see page 197 at the back of this book and explore its website: [www.heifer.org].

There Is Another Way Of Living And Being

Society taught us to live in a certain way, but, for many of us, it is not working. We sense this failure because we suffer too much from anxiety and stress. There is a quiet longing for a greater sense of well-being and contentment. What society taught us is the old way. *The Woo Way* offers us a choice to think and live in a new way. It is based on four simple principles: Expand and deepen awareness, from that growing awareness make new choices, from those choices develop new practices, then use those practices to make changes in the way you think and live.

The Woo Way is a play on the words "Wu Wei" in Taoism, which Benjamin Hoff describes in *The Tao of Pooh:*

> When you work with Wu Wei, you put the round peg in the round hole and the square peg in the square hole. No stress, no struggle. Egotistical Desire tries to force the round peg into the square hole and the square peg in the round hole. Cleverness tries to devise craftier ways of making pegs fit where they don't belong. Knowledge tries to figure out why the round pegs fit round holes, but not square holes. Wu Wei doesn't try. It doesn't think about it. It just does it. And when it does, it doesn't appear to do much of

anything. But Things Get Done. (Hoff, p. 75)

The Woo Way could be called the "Whew Way," like "What a relief!", the "Wo-o-o-o Way," the recovery of wonder, or the "Woo-e-e-e Way," the development of playfulness. Each of these meanings captures something about the Woo Way as an option to the way we normally think and live. It must cultivate playfulness if it is to be in Woo, for Woo is the state where the opposites counterbalance each other in the tension of wholeness.

A Woo Master would say, "Hold 'serious' in one hand, 'playful' in other. Watch life become easier." Within each of us there is a Woo Master who symbolizes our wholeness and wisdom. Since our tendency is to think in terms of male or female, either way of identifying the Woo Master's gender is fine. It can be a man or woman, depending on your preference. It may even be a child. Goldilocks in "Goldilocks and the Three Bears" appears as a Woo Master because she operates with the idea of "just right." She chooses the porridge that is neither too hot nor too cold, the chair that is neither too big nor too little, the bed that is neither too hard nor too soft. Balance is what she seeks because she knows that works best.

In the comments of the Woo Master scattered throughout the book, you will notice variations of English grammar, especially the absence of "the" and "a". This takes the Woo Master's words out of the realm of the ordinary to stand as examples of universal wisdom. It integrates what has been divided, balancing East, West, North, and South to form a circle. The style of speaking is intended to reflect this balance, harmony, and wholeness. The Woo Master encourages flexibility in the way you think about and try to change your life.

Woo Master:
"Woo is way to live in balance with knees bent.
Easy to go this way or that way.
People will ask, why is that person so unruffled?
Simple. Balanced with knees bent."

Two little words are essential for understanding the Woo Way. The first is "Too," as in "too much" and "too little." This word helps us to understand when we are out of balance. "Too much control" will get us in trouble as much as exercising "too little control." The other little word is "Two." It suggests the presence of the opposites within our thinking and learning to live between them. When we create balance, we live between the two extremes. *The Woo Way* is about learning to attain that balance in order to achieve more wholeness of being.

I have been privileged to offer the teachings of *The Woo Way* to students at the University of Colorado in Boulder for many years. While most of my students have been in their twenties, others have been in their thirties, forties, or fifties. You will become aware of their changes by reading excerpts from their stories throughout the book. Out of respect for them, I have changed their names to conceal their identities.

The Woo Way makes its way out of the classroom and into your hands with the hope that the work you undertake will enhance the quality of your life. Sharing the work is part of my four simple life purposes: To help others reduce their suffering, enhance their well-being, and increase their creativity, then to do all those things for myself.

There are four parts of the work: "Living In Automatic," "Everyone Is Telling Stories," "Making Relationships Work," and "Developing Balance, Wholeness, and Wisdom." Each part has a unique focus and the chapters reveal important issues as we seek awareness, choice, and change. You will be doing experiential processes, so please purchase a large journal to record your work. In "Making Relationships Work," we will be exploring psychological types. You will need to take a test to learn about your type. You can do this either in David Keirsey, *Please Understand Me II* or David Keirsey and Marilyn Bates, *Please Understand Me*. If you have internet access, the test can be completed and you can learn about your type at [http://Keirsey.com/]. Another option is to take the Myers-Briggs Personality Inventory. Many counseling centers administer this test.

While this book can be done alone with good results, I highly recommend that you do it with others. There is value in working with a partner or a group of people. Group work reveals how most of us are dealing with the same issues. There is comfort in knowing that. It is also a wonderful way to develop community.

There are different approaches to the work. The best option is to do it from cover to cover, because the processes are sequential, with one learning experience leading to the next. You can choose the work you want to do by first checking the summaries of the chapters in the Contents. You could decide to start with the section of the book that most appeals to you. A single chapter can make a difference, depending on your needs and your willingness to use the teaching in your life. Practicing the lessons of each chapter will give you an idea of what you want to integrate into your life.

I invite you into this work, hoping that it will nourish your life as well as the lives of those your changes touch. At the very least, it might put a little smile on your face.

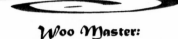

Woo Master:
"To see more clearly,
turn up inner light."

Visit the Life Gardening Project on the Web at:
[http://lifegardening.com].

Part I

Living In Automatic

*T*his part of the work deals with our conditioning and how we compensate for feelings of inadequacy. Not wanting to feel little and bad, we develop strategies for managing the size of our egos. How and why we do that is revealed in the following chapters. By discovering what controls us automatically, we are able to make choices and change. More freedom is the outcome.

Chapter 1

You Have The Power To Change

"**I** want to survive" is perhaps the most primal admission human beings can make. To help us survive, nature has equipped us with the ability to distinguish between what is threatening and safe. These calculations are often so subtle, we may not notice how much attention we pay to our survival each day. A part of our survival revolves around the need to compensate for the feelings of inadequacy we developed while growing up. Those feelings emerged quite naturally from the way we were socialized.

Most of us embrace the idea that there is something wrong with us that needs fixing. Sensing our inadequacy, we have moments when we feel small, which makes us feel bad. Since we dislike feeling that way, we put a lot of effort into managing the size of our egos to feel better. We will learn about what makes us feel little and what methods we employ to feel good.

We grow up believing we are free, but we think and behave in automatic ways, like machines. When we understand our conditioning, we establish the possibility of greater autonomy to choose and to change. We can decide to try new approaches, embrace new ideas, and remodel ourselves so our suffering is reduced and our well-being is enhanced. By exercising our capacity for choice, we deal with our feelings of inadequacy and find a way to recover our balance. Since choice is always available, so is the possibility of change.

Through our choices, we shape ourselves and our lives.
Each person and each life is a work of art.
Choice shapes how the art forms and evolves.

When I was in my late thirties, I had an important insight. It was so crucial I have been living in it ever since. It was the realization that I was born to see how far I could take my personal development in my lifetime. I established a guiding question: "How much can I change over the remaining years of my life, so I become a comfortable home to myself others will enjoy visiting?" This is an inner career where remodeling never ends. What kind of person do you want to be when you are eighty? Someone with a quiet smile and soft eyes or someone with a rigid face and harsh attitude? What will you need to change within yourself to still be smiling and peaceful at the end?

Woo Master:
"Knowing our destination helps get us there."

Individual Process (5 minutes): On a journal page, write some guiding questions you might want your life to serve as you consider remodeling yourself over the rest of your life time.

Circle the question that expresses your deepest life purpose.

Recess of the mind: Close your eyes and reflect on your guiding question and how it gives your life purpose and direction.

If you are working with a partner or group, share your guiding questions.

You already have the ability to remodel yourself. In the past, you undoubtedly created changes that made you feel better about yourself and your life. You also learned to accept what you once rejected. What led you to make those changes?

The desire to remodel a house arises from the awareness that something needs to be changed. Perhaps there is not ample room or enough light. The same may be true about what motivates us to remodel ourselves. Our suffering helps us to discover what to change. When you understand what is making you suffer, you can remodel your thinking and the situation to reduce it. When suffering appears, you can respond, "It's remodeling time! What new choices can I make to change the situation? What new practices can I try?" In designing a simple strategy for remodeling yourself, deepening your awareness, making new choices, and starting new practices are key ideas to keep in mind.

■ Notice what is not working. Become keenly aware of the suffering and what is causing it.

■ Focus on how your thinking and behavior contribute to your suffering. Avoid blaming yourself. You are the only person over which you have any real control. It is easier to change yourself than to change others.

■ Generate options for remodeling. What specific things

could be changed or accepted? This is where creativity can help you generate ideas as you seek to make alterations of yourself. Accepting what cannot be changed is one way to make a change.

■ Design your remodel. Decide what to incorporate into your remodeling project, including what you want to change and accept. How do you want the finished product to look? Imagine the change already made.

■ Practice the new way of thinking or being until it is fully integrated. Remodeling is achieved by continuous awareness, choice, and practice.

In terms of learning, suffering is superior to any book. It is a call for change.

Individual Process (30 minutes): In the middle of a journal page, write "What is causing me to suffer?" Around the page, note the causes of your suffering.

Circle any suffering that is urgently calling you to do some inner remodeling. From among those items, select one suffering as the focus of your work. Divide a new page into quarters. At the top, write the suffering you are going to explore. Enter one of the following questions in each part.

■ "How do my thinking and behavior contribute to this suffering?"

■ "What options exist for changing my thinking and behavior?"

■ "What specifically do I choose to change?"

■ "How will I put the change into practice?"

Write an answer to each question in the order presented.

When you have completed your work, close your eyes. Imagine yourself practicing your changes until they have become part of the way you are and live. See the remodeling completed.

If you are working with a partner or group, share your insights.

Sometimes little changes produce big results.

Patience And Practice Are Important

In seeking change, it is wise to be patient and take our time, otherwise the remodeling becomes an ordeal. The Woo Master would say: "Small steps get us there without tiring." By seeing change as your inner career, you give yourself time to accomplish your goals. In this less harried effort, practice becomes crucial, however many years you have left for the work. Something new comes into being when it replaces what is not working. Practice produces that change.

One way to understand the importance of practice is to consider becoming more proficient in a sport such as tennis. If you have played tennis for a few years and decide to take lessons, several things will happen. Your coach will point out bad habits that you have developed which make you less effective as a player. Then you will learn how to break those habits. This will include changes in the way you move, hold your racket, stroke the ball, and approach strategy. If you want to improve your game, you must practice the new techniques diligently. If you fail to practice, your game will remain as it was before.

It is the same with this inner work. If you fail to develop new life practices for yourself, then employ them conscientiously, you will remain as you were. Awareness, choice, and practice are the essential ingredients for success in making personal changes. As in tennis, practice is the hardest, most crucial part of the work.

Many people have little patience for practice, so they avoid it. They may want the quick result without making much effort. Without practice, there are no results. While diligent practice is essential, it does not have to become an obsession. Try, but not so hard that you make yourself miserable. When you relax and make steady efforts to change, it becomes like a shopping trip where, not feeling pressured to buy, you discover exactly what you want.

Woo Master:
"In practice, I keep smile on face.
Smile is friend saying
'Try, but not too hard'."

Mitchell was in emotional turmoil when he took my class. He was lonely and suffered from self-doubt and internal conflicts about his past. Behind this emotional storm that swept over him was a young man who showed enormous potential for understanding and wisdom. He had depth, compassion, and a wealth of experience for a man in his twenties. As he moved through this work, he realized its value and moved into practice. His practice was steady and diligent, but not frantic, so soon he was getting results. By the end of the term, he had made important changes in his thinking and identity. His life began to work with much less effort. A lighter spirit replaced his troubling moods.

After graduation, Mitchell moved away, so I lost contact with him. Two years later, he came back for a visit and stopped to see me. He was still in conscientious practice, so his life was working even better than when I had last seen him. He was free from many of his internal struggles and was living with greater ease and effectiveness. As he talked, I could hear wisdom in his words. Through practice, he had created a balanced way of living and being.

8-30-11

Chapter 2

Ideals Have Teeth

Most of the judgments we make each day are guided by ideals we developed or that were instilled in us by our parents, teachers, clergy, friends, and the media. Ideals are beliefs that affect our attitudes about the way social life should be, including how we should treat each other, dress, think, look, and behave. Ideals are necessary for an ordered society. They shape social norms and help regulate social life so it is manageable, relatively free, and safe. They are the basis for kindness, compassion, nonviolence, and cooperation within the moral order.

Our ideals are developed so gradually, we lose awareness of having learned them. Yet, they strongly shape our daily choices and behavior. When ideals are too lofty, they have sharp teeth so they cause us emotional pain, in moments of disappointment, self-condemnation, guilt, or depression. Unaware of how our ideals make us suffer, we never pause to explore and question them. When we do, we may discover some ideals we would honor for their moral value. Others of less moral consequence we might change, if they make us suffer.

———————

Woo Master:
*"When I build wall too high,
I make climb over very difficult."*

Perfectionists are most prone to build high walls and have to make difficult climbs because of their high ideals. Being one of these perfectionists, Denise had ideals with very sharp teeth. She constantly criticized herself for not being good enough, others for failing to treat each other well, and society for not caring about the fate of individuals. As she became aware of the power of ideals to inflict pain, she realized how much she suffered because her ideals were too lofty. The standards she had set for herself, others, and society were so unrealistic, there was no way they would ever be achieved. With such high ideals, she was constantly disappointed, guilty, critical, and depressed.

"Ideals Have Teeth" made her realize how she set up the conditions for her own suffering. Her ideals were so out of balance with reality, her only hope was to alter her ideals. She explored them carefully, deciding which ones to keep, modify, and discard. Gradually, she found a way to have ideals without such sharp teeth. At that point, her suffering declined and she was able to move into more positive avenues of life. It took courage to do what she did, because she had to undo a perfectionist fantasy that had gripped her whole life.

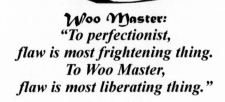

Woo Master:
"To perfectionist,
flaw is most frightening thing.
To Woo Master,
flaw is most liberating thing."

Some of us have ideals with sharp teeth like Denise's that persistently make us suffer. Other ideals have teeth, but they are not so sharp. Some ideals, if they are within easier reach, might have no teeth at all. You will have an opportunity to become more aware of your ideals and discover if any have sharp teeth. From that awareness, you may decide to so some remodeling.

Individual Process (30 minutes): Our ideals appear as "shoulds" in our thinking. If you want to identify your ideals, notice what you keep telling yourself about how you or others should look, think, and behave.

Divide a journal page into four parts. Write one of the following statements in each part.

"Ideals about how my body should look." (Example: "I should have nice-looking skin.")

"Ideals about personal qualities I should have." ("I should be confident.")

"Ideals about how I should behave." ("I should be nice to people and other animals.")

"Ideals about how others should behave or treat me." ("They should be kind.")

Note your ideals in each area. These should be your ideals, which may be different from the ideals society wants you to embrace.

Circle the ideals with the sharpest teeth. Taking each of those ideals in turn, close your eyes and contemplate how they cause you to suffer when they are unrealized.

Move into choice. Examine each ideal with sharp teeth and make a choice about it, as if your life were beginning now.

What ideals would you choose to throw out? Cross those

out.

What ideals would you remodel? Circle those. Take one and remodel it. "I should be confident" could be remodeled into "I should strive to be confident, but it's okay to lack confidence at times."

What ideals would you keep as they are? Put stars by those.

What new ideals would you like to add? Include those.

If you are working with a partner or group, share your discoveries and choices.

What if this moment were the beginning of your life? How would you shape your ideals to reduce your suffering and increase your happiness?

Chapter 3

I Want To Look Good
And Be Accepted

When I was a new college professor, I felt intellectually inadequate because I knew so little. This meant that I was constantly trying to impress others with my intelligence. To look good, I worked hard to display my knowledge and win arguments. I was competitive. I tried to finish any discussion in the superior position. Being right and looking good at the end was my goal. To achieve that objective, I sometimes exaggerated and deceived to impress others. For example, when asked if I had read a particular book, I would say "Yes" when I had not read it. Perhaps you know someone who behaves this way. Maybe you are that someone.

We all do things like that. It is part of human nature. We want to look good and fear looking bad. We want to be right. We want to be strong and independent. In the next few chapters, we will explore the ways we try to feel good about ourselves.

The ideas we will cover are so simple, you may be tempted to rush through them. Yet, their simplicity is what makes them powerful explanations for how we think and interact with others in conditioned ways. Reaching adulthood, we may believe we are beyond the issues that drove us to distraction during adolescence. In reality, we are often preoccupied with the same issues, even into old age. Two of the big issues we face every day are wanting to look good and be accepted. We are constantly trying to impress others so they will like us.

I Am Afraid of Looking Foolish

In class, I open the work about looking good by wearing a funny wig and a plastic pig snout. Students immediately feel awkward, not knowing how to interact with me. After a few minutes of looking ridiculous, I ask if someone would be willing to don the wig and snout. Usually, there is a brave soul who will try it. The last time it was John, a man in his forties. With wig and snout in place, he stood in front of fifty people trying not to be nervous. Within ten seconds, his face became red, giving away his inner anxiety and fear.

Looking bad automatically produces this kind of embarrassment. If you want to directly experience what I mean, buy a funny wig and plastic snout, put them on, and walk down a busy street. You will be embarrassed and it will be a response to something that controls human beings automatically. We want to look good and fear looking bad.

Notice how many times a day you look in the mirror to make sure your image is presentable, so you will make a good impression. When you succeed and someone compliments you, it makes you feel good. Remember how terrible you felt when a hair cut turned bad and you had to appear in public afterwards. You probably struggled to maintain your confidence. Recall the time when you came home from a party to discover a piece of lettuce stuck in your front teeth. Even after the fact, you probably felt embarrassed for looking foolish. Wanting to look good occupies a good deal of our attention and it is automatic. You will start noticing how much time we put into this effort. It is amazing and amusing.

Woo Master:
"Afraid of looking silly,
you lose freedom to be silly."

Individual Process (20 minutes): On a journal page, draw a large stick figure with eyes, nose, ears, and mouth. The figure will represent you and your attempts to look good. Some of your efforts may be related to body image, how you adorn yourself, how you behave, and what you say. Write about your efforts to look good, drawing a line to the part of your body where those attempts occur. If you try to appear smart to look good, you would draw a line to your head. If you smile a lot to look good, drawn a line to your mouth.

When you have completed noting what you do to look good, circle any item where there is a nagging and persistent fear of looking foolish or inadequate. This will make you aware of what aspects of looking good most control you. If your appearance is extremely important, you will be constantly vigilant about how your face and body look. If you are afraid people will think you are unfriendly, you will live in the tension of a forced smile.

Somewhere near your figure, note one or two key strategies you employ to look good. Do you "play it safe" by being cautious with words, dress, and behavior? Are you excessively friendly?

How do your strategies limit you? What parts of yourself do you sacrifice by using them? The "play it safe" approach would cause someone to sacrifice honesty and full self-expression.

What new choices would you like to make?

What will you do differently now?

If you are working with a partner or group, reveal what you learned.

Woo Master:
"Life is best opportunity to be ourselves."

When new choices and practices are undertaken, we take a risk. Under such circumstances, courage, curiosity, and the desire for adventure are helpful. Brenda discovered this. I could not help noticing her on the first day of class. She was striking, with radiant dark hair, large brown eyes, and a full, beautifully shaped mouth. Then, I noticed the make-up. Her eyes were heavily lined with dark mascara and her lips were carefully painted with bright red lipstick. She was exquisitely crafted. She must have spent an hour preparing her image.

Every day Brenda appeared covered by her mask of heavy make-up. Then one day I noticed a visitor sitting in the front row. I was about to welcome her, when I realized to my surprise that it was Brenda. She had no make-up on, so I had not recognized her. I observed that she was still attractive, but no longer strikingly beautiful. I asked her why she was not wearing make-up. "Experiment" she said with a big smile. Smiling myself, I said nothing more. She had recognized her strategies for looking good and had taken a

grip on her fears. I knew what she was doing was courageous, because she was consciously taking the risk of looking bad. She was trying to move out of automatic into
choice about wanting to look good. I was impressed.

I observed Brenda's experiment with great interest. After
class one day, she spoke to me about it. "I've realized that
I need to wear make-up because it makes me feel better.
When I don't, I feel exposed and weak. Now I understand
how human I'm being about this and, knowing that, I can
wear make-up without feeling guilty." What a nice realization! She could be merely human and live freely within
that.

She also made a change. She began using less make-up. By
the end of the term, she had softened the hard, dark lines of
mascara around her eyes, so they were subtle rather than
glaring and obvious. She also toned down the striking color
of her lipstick. When I first saw her in heavy make-up, I
thought to myself: "There's a young woman who's uncomfortable with her appearance." By simply toning down the
extreme intensity of her make-up, she produced a dramatic
change in the way others perceived her. By finding a better
balance in the application of her make-up, she no longer
conveyed a sense of inadequacy about her appearance.
Thus, she appeared as an attractive and self-confident person. She had heeded the Wooish principle: "What we take
to extreme works against us."

Please Accept Me

Our attempts to look good in the opinion of others have an
ulterior motive. If we look good, we increase our chances
of being accepted. In social life, the value of an individual
is determined by the evaluation of others. Since we under-

stand this, we are constantly trying to impress people so they see us as worthy and say so in public. Public acclaim is one of the things that makes us feel special. When we observe ourselves closely, it becomes apparent how much effort goes into seeking acceptance. If we succeed in being accepted, we feel good.

Individual Process (30 minutes): In your journal, identify the names of people from whom you want acceptance and briefly describe what you do to achieve it. For example, "I want my boss to accept me. To achieve her acceptance, I respond immediately to her wishes."

Circle the names of those from whom you most want acceptance. Why? How does that shape your life and choices?

From whom do you most fear rejection? How do you avoid being rejected by them? How does that affect your life and choices?

What are one or two key strategies you use to gain acceptance or avoid rejection? For example, are you excessively nice or do you withhold sensitive information about yourself?

How do those strategies limit you? What parts of yourself do you sacrifice?

What new choices would you like to make?

What will you do differently now as a practice?

If you are working with a partner or group, share what you just discovered.

*The person from whom we most fear rejection is often
the person we try hardest to impress and please.
Our fear gives that person control over us.*

After the class completed this work about looking good and
seeking acceptance, a hand went up in the back of the classroom. It was Jonathan. "Every day when I return home,
my face hurts because I've been smiling so much. By smiling, I'm trying to tell others that I'm happy and friendly so
they'll like and accept me. Today, I realized what a burden
this has been for me. I need to ask you all a question: 'If I
quit smiling when I don't feel like it, will you still accept
me?'" A resounding "Yes" went up from the group.
Jonathan smiled and it was genuine.

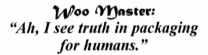

Woo Master:
*"Ah, I see truth in packaging
for humans."*

By understanding what you do to feel good about yourself,
you can relax and decide to be human without regret or
resistance. Knowing you cannot help wanting to look good
and be liked, you acknowledge your nature and experiment
as Brenda did with her make-up. You can also choose to
make a change by trying other ways of thinking and being,
like deciding to follow Jonathan's example and quit smiling
all the time. Both approaches can reduce your suffering and
give you greater access to freedom. Playing with being
human, your life will lighten up a bit.

*Wanting to feel special,
human beings dislike being merely human.*

Chapter 4

I Want Independence And Control

*W*hile jockeying for autonomy and advantage is part of the game of everyday life, admitting that we crave independence and control may be hard. Yet, exerting independence and taking the upper hand may be our favorite strategies for feeling good about ourselves. When given an opportunity to exercise independence and control, our mood may suddenly improve. In contrast, if circumstances cause us to feel overly dependent or controlled, humiliation or anger may sweep through us to ruin a good day. Some people are more in the grip of these issues than others. For them, life may become a battle and proving ground.

Woo Master:
*"When struggle stops,
playing begins."*

I Crave Independence

"Don't fence me in" is a western ballad that captures the American notion that dependence on another person can become like a prison to escape. In contrast, independence is a way to establish and maintain control over our options.

While many couples work their way through these issues and find a nice balance between dependence and independence as they age together, some do not. Even into the last stages of life, a couple can struggle over these issues.

Men have a long-standing desire to prove their independence. Yet, women can also be adamant about claiming their autonomy and personal power after years of discrimination. Like men, they may rebel when a relationship infringes on their independence. Elaine described how she entered relationships madly in love, then looked for a quick exit when she began feeling dependent on her mate. This happened over and over, so she had many flings but no deep relationships. "The moment I felt dependent, I began to experience panic, like I was losing myself. As soon as I began feeling that way, I'd become difficult, find many problems in the relationship, and rationalize my way out of it."

People can become so dependent on their independence that they lose their balance.

Individual Process (30 minutes): Write a brief letter to a young child about the issues of dependence and independence. Imagine giving the child instructions about what she or he must learn and do about dependence and independence to have a successful life. Be spontaneous in writing the letter and sincere about preparing the child for the future.

When your letter is finished, examine it as messages about independence and dependence that have guided your life for years. Underline those messages, then write briefly about how they have affected your thinking and behavior about autonomy. If you are not following your advice, write about what would change in your life if you did.

Given what you see, note one or two leading strategies you use to deal with the issues of independence and dependence.

How have those strategies limited you? What part of yourself have you sacrificed?

How have those strategies affected your relationships?

What new choices would you like to make?

What new practice will you try?

Write a brief letter to yourself reflecting your decisions about these issues.

If you are working with a partner or group, read your letters to each other and share your insights.

When you are able to choose independence or dependence at appropriate times, your capacity to strengthen a relationship increases. Through dependence, you learn to rely on the other person to satisfy some of your needs, which helps you and gives that person's life greater meaning. Through independence, you learn to rely on yourself and to have your own interests. In the relationship, your lives become intertwined but separate. You enjoy time together and apart. Because mutual needs for independence and dependence are honored, you appreciate each other and the relationship.

Woo Master:
"Balance dependence and independence,
then relationship works.
No big effort. No big fuss."

I Need Control

Observe young children for an hour. Notice how they try to get control when they feel there is something at stake. They learn early that crying annoys their parents and they use it as a resource to get what they want. The temper tantrum is their last desperate effort to see if their parents will cave in to their demands. Parents must learn to resist giving in to the tantrum. As children, we all tried the tantrum tactic. When other attempts fail, some of us still use it to get our way. Pouting and withdrawal are also used by some adults. Others argue to gain dominance. Seeking revenge is a common practice when all methods of control have failed. These are blatant attempts to establish control when there is something at stake, but we also employ many subtle strategies like compliments, negotiation, and persuasion.

Having something at stake is what drives people to seek control of choices in a situation. When we have a strong motivation to achieve a result, our control muscles are flexed. When there is no stake, we may let others get their way. Power struggles occur when two or more people have high stakes in the same situation.

Woo Master:
"Tense grip, tense mind.
Tense mind, tense life."

Individual Process (20 minutes): On small pieces of paper, briefly note strategies you employ to get your way in situations that matter to you. Make sure to include your subtle methods.

When your strategies have been fully noted, lay them out in front of you. Organize them into a pattern that reflects the frequency of their use.

Among your tactics, identify one or two strategies you use often. For example, "I argue my point with such passion that it overwhelms the other person's resistance."

How do those key strategies limit you? What part of you is denied?

What new choices would you like to make?

What will you introduce as a new practice?

If you are working with a partner or group, share what you learned and what new choices you made.

> *If we are addicted to control, we are never*
> *completely happy with our results*
> *because we know the addiction is*
> *controlling us.*

By reclaiming aspects of themselves they have sacrificed, many people doing this work become aware that they are moving closer to the balance point within themselves. With this shift toward the center, they begin to grasp the wisdom of Goldilocks and her search for "just right." When we achieve more balance, our lives begin to work on an even keel and with less effort. Suddenly, we discover the Woo Master within us.

"I'm the Woo Master," Meg declared one day.

"What do you mean?" I asked.

"As I make choices to live in the middle of many of these issues, not going too far one way or the other, I've realized that it's me who's creating my own balance. I'm the Woo Master."

"So, what would your Woo Master say about your discovery?"

"The Woo Master in me would smile that little smile and say 'About time'."

Chapter 5

I Want To Be Right

If we could observe ourselves during an argument, it would become apparent how automatically we try to be right and not wrong about facts and beliefs. Sometimes, we will fight over the most trivial fact, because it makes us feel good to be right, while being wrong diminishes our feeling of worth. We are often self-righteous about our moral values, knowing that those who disagree with us must be inferior. Being right establishes control, but also a sense of certainty in our minds, which helps us avoid troubling doubts and confusion about life and reality.

Would you be annoyed if someone said they were right and you were wrong? At some level, we are all making this statement. There are essentially three things humans want to be right about: Facts (which are verifiable), beliefs, and moral values. In the following work, you will focus on your beliefs and moral values.

Individual Process (30 minutes): Divide a journal page in half. In one part, indicate the beliefs you want to be right about. For example, "There is an afterlife" or "There isn't."

Note one or two key strategies you employ to convince people that you are right and not wrong about your beliefs. For example, "I become insistent that my view is correct."

In the other part, note the moral values you want to be right about. For example, "People should be kind to each other."

Record one or two crucial strategies you use to insure that you are right and not wrong about your values. For example, "I try to make other people feel guilty for what they believe."

In pursuing your strategies, what part of yourself do you sacrifice?

Now, you will do a mind stretch, so you will have to be flexible. Reexamine the writing you have done about the beliefs and values you want to be right about. Select an important one from each category. Taking each in turn, describe how you are wrong about it. Be convincing.

If you are working with a partner or group, try to convince your partner or group that you are wrong about the beliefs and values that you identified. Take turns. Be convincing. Discuss what you learned.

If it becomes rigid, our insistence on being right about our beliefs and values prevents us from seeing other possibilities. This works against balance.

If you are like others who have done this work, you failed to convince yourself that you were wrong about your beliefs and values. You may have become angry or abandoned the process because you knew you were right.

Individual Process (5 minutes): I want you to know: "You are wrong." What feelings arise when you hear that? Note those in your journal.

From that experience, what do you now understand about human beings and yourself?

Given that understanding, what new choices do you want to make?

What will you do differently now?

If you are working with a partner or group, reveal what you learned.

Woo Master:
"Between loose and rigid, Woo lives.
Flexible, it enjoys doubt as
playful dance between opposites."

Doubt makes us uncomfortable. Certainty makes us feel secure and at home. Our egos feel good when we are clear that we know. Even when we do not know, we are likely to make up a story about knowing. This is so automatic that we fail to notice how often we doubt the truth of what we are saying. Sometimes, the declaration that some belief or value is true entrenches us to a point where it becomes true for us, despite evidence to the contrary. Mental rigidity sets in and we lose the doubt that could put us in balance.

I asked Julie one day how she was doing.

"Not so well. I'm so confused."

"Well, you're a short step from enlightenment," I responded.

"What do you mean?"

"Enlightenment occurs when you're confused and you don't worry about it anymore."

Not knowing, being confused, and feeling uncertain about the truth makes us more open to new ideas and less likely to create enemies of others who hold different views.

Woo Master:
"Doubt keeps doors of mind open."

Chapter 6

ℐ 𝒩eed 𝒥o 𝒻eel 𝒮afe

An interesting letter appeared in an advice column from a woman who loved to hug her favorite stuffed animal while falling asleep. Her new husband encouraged her. The woman described his support as liberating, because she was given permission to take care of her need for security. Most of us would not carry our favorite stuffed animal around each day to feel secure, yet we constantly create sanctuaries of safety. Even risk takers place limits on what they will try. Given our primal mission of survival, everyone pays attention to security, but some of us pay more attention to it than others.

Fear is a common occurrence in our minds. We strive to look good, but fear looking bad. We fear rejection and failure. We fear being dependent, losing control, and being wrong. We fear insecurity. In fact, we are afraid of fear. At a deep level, fear runs us all. In the shadow of our daily lives, fear lurks as nagging worries, making us cautious as we manage our lives and our thinking so we can feel secure enough to function in a healthy way. This is an inescapable part of being human and not anything to feel guilty about. When our fears are more fully known, managing them becomes easier. Instead of worrying so much, life becomes more of an adventure.

For people who live with many fears, the obsession to feel safe may be so great, their lives become frozen. Suzanne described this problem: "I'm so fearful of something going wrong that I'm constantly trying to feel safe. This has become a nightmare for me, because I've become so cautious I have a hard time making decisions and I'm always worried about how others will judge me." Suzanne's despair arises from the fact that she is out of balance about needing so much security, but the opposite tendency can also produce problems. Someone who never worries, who takes unnecessary risks, can also get into trouble.

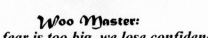

Woo Master:
*"When fear is too big, we lose confidence.
When too small, we feel invincible.
Danger in both places."*

Individual Process (25 minutes): At the top of a journal page, list your security-oriented fears, leaving some space between them.

Next, after each fear, note your strategy for dealing with it.

Examining your strategies, identify the ones you use most often.

How do those strategies limit you? What part of you is denied when you use them?

What new choices would you like to make?

What new practice will you create?

If you are working with a partner or group, share your discoveries and choices.

Although carrying a favorite stuffed animal around for security may not be possible, paying attention to your fears and needs for security is a good idea. When insecurity appears, you may feel weak and inadequate. When your needs for security are admitted, it is easier to balance wanting security with your willingness to take a risk. This balance keeps your creative options open. At that point, your life becomes more of an adventure, but not such a frightening one that you become immobilized.

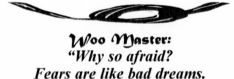

Woo Master:
"Why so afraid?
Fears are like bad dreams.
Seldom come true."

What Issues Have The Strongest Grip On You?

"I hate this work," Joel cried out one day in class.

"What's the problem?" was my quick response.

"I thought I'd grown beyond these issues, that I'd evolved since I was a teenager. I hate realizing that, not only am I dealing with the same issues, but there's probably not a complete escape from them. Human beings are so stuck, what hope is there?"

"Can you laugh about it?" I asked.

"Not yet."

"Keep working until quiet laughter emerges, then you'll understand the Woo Master's words, 'When smile emerges, liberation is at door'."

Some aspects of what controls human beings automatically may have a more compelling influence on us than others. Being right may dominate us. Wanting control or needing security may be our chief preoccupations. Which issues have the tightest grip on you?

Individual Process (10 minutes): Check one or two of the following issues that have the strongest hold on you.

☐ Want to look good and be accepted; afraid of looking bad and rejection.

☐ Want independence and control; afraid of dependence and loss of control.

☐ Want to be right; afraid of being wrong.

☐ Want to feel secure: Afraid of insecurity.

What are one or two key strategies that you consistently use to deal with your most gripping issues?

Seeing those strategies, what prospects for change do you notice?

If you are working with a partner or group, discuss what you found and what you want to change. Remember, small changes can produce big results.

Dawn realized that she spent most of her daily effort seeking acceptance from others. Her key strategy for gaining their approval was to be excessively nice. It worked, but she sacrificed her independent spirit. She chose to reduce her efforts to gain acceptance and to focus her time on cultivating more independence. To achieve that new goal, she established a practice. "Every time I become aware that I'm seeking acceptance, I'll focus on my desire for full self expression." Based on her increased willingness to face rejection, this practice freed her to state her opinions more openly and honestly. She created a better balance between wanting to please others and needing to please herself.

You will need two balloons for the next chapter.

Chapter 7

Restoring A Shrinking Ego

When someone compliments us for a job well done, our ego becomes bigger and happiness miraculously appears. In that state of euphoria, the world seems like a beautiful place. In contrast, harsh words can produce a temporary collapse of the ego, causing us to fall into a dark depression. Our ego's size constantly fluctuates as it reacts to how we are treated, the extent of our successes and blunders, and how well our performances come off. Expansion and contraction, expansion and contraction, expansion and contraction: No wonder we are tired at the end of a day!

After missing one of my classes, Margie explained that a professor had criticized her during a class session that morning. I asked her how it made her feel. "So small and terrible, I went home and went to bed." Because someone criticized her ideas, her ego collapsed. We all experience this at times. Rejection is likely to bring it on. We might also notice our ego shrinking after learning about a friend's success.

Egos Expand And Contract

Compliments and criticisms are two sides of the same coin; both show how we automatically react to what others say to us or about us.

Preparatory Process for Individuals, Partners, or a Group (15 minutes): Tear up a piece of paper into eight parts. You will write a statement on each piece of paper covering both sides of the four issues we have explored.

Wanting to look good and be accepted versus looking bad and being rejected: What could someone say to you, or to others about you, that would make you look good or feel accepted? Write it down. On a second slip, record a statement that would make you look bad or feel rejected.

Wanting independence and control versus being dependent and losing control: What could some say to you that would make you feel independent or in control? Note it. On another slip, write what could be said to you that would make you feel dependent or without control.

Wanting to be right versus being wrong: What could someone say that would make you feel that you were right? What words would make you feel wrong? Write those statements on separate slips.

Want security versus insecurity: What could someone say to you that would make you feel secure? What statement would make you insecure? Note those on separate slips.

Individual Process (20 minutes): Take your eight statements, turn them over, and mix them thoroughly. Blow up a balloon until it is as big as the ego size that feels good to you, not the size you ideally want it to be.

Begin by turning over a statement, then read it aloud as if someone were speaking directly to you. Notice your emotional reaction when you hear the statement. If your ego would normally deflate upon hearing the words, release air from the balloon to represent how much your ego's size would diminish. If the statement would make your ego feel bigger, blow air into the balloon until it grows as large as your ego under those circumstances. As you move through your slips, release or add air to your balloon to reflect your emotional response to each statement.

Since your slips of paper are mixed, you may get a string of bad luck or good news, which is often the way life occurs. Your balloon may become enormous or lose all of its air. If you have a string of positive statements, it may pop, so have another balloon on hand. Notice these mood swings in your life. There are times when our egos become pitifully small because nothing is working right but, when everything is going our way, they can become quite large.

Process for Partners or a Group (30 minutes): If you are working in a group, select a partner to work with. The partners exchange statements. The statements are turned face down and mixed. Each partner blows up a balloon until it represents a reasonably sized ego. Decide who will be "A" and "B." "A" will start, but "A" and "B" will take turns throughout the process.

"B" turns over one of "A's" slips and makes the statement to "A" as it might be said under normal circumstances. (This may be difficult because most of us dislike saying things to people that we know will make them feel bad. Yet, we help each other practice by creating as realistic a situation as possible.) "A" either inflates or deflates the balloon according to whether the statement makes the ego feel bigger or smaller. Then, "A" turns over one of "B's" slips and communicates the message with conviction to "B." "B" adds or subtracts air from the balloon, reflecting what would happen to the size of the ego after hearing that message. As you move randomly through the statements, notice how periods of good news and bad affect the size of your ego.

When you have finished, share with each other what you noticed and learned. If you are working in a group, come together to share and discuss your experiences. Someone from the group should guide and pace the sharing process, so there is enough time for the following work.

Using "Recovery Claims"

Many peoples' lives are like a roller coaster, with steep climbs and falls. These sudden changes are the result of the ego expanding and contracting as it reacts emotionally to what life serves them. Is there an alternative to this dynamic, but sometimes agonizing, shift between exhilaration and depression? Is there anything you can do to bolster your ego before it crashes?

You can establish a "recovery claim," which is a positive statement about yourself that you know is true. This claim will help you stop your ego from collapsing when circumstances trigger a deflation. By asserting your claim, your ego will never become so tiny and depressed that, like Margie, you have to take it home and put it to bed.

When your ego has enlarged, how do you feel?

(Check one)

☐ Inadequate
☐ Barely adequate
☐ Good enough
☐ Good
☐ Very good
☐ Perfect

When your ego has become small, how do you feel?

(Check one)

☐ Inadequate
☐ Barely adequate
☐ Good enough
☐ Good
☐ Very good
☐ Perfect

When your ego is shrinking, what choice would you make on the scale above to restore its size? Put a check by that choice. Typically, people select "good enough" or "good." Those choices can be converted into recovery claims to keep the ego from collapsing. "I'm good enough," "I'm a good person," or "I will learn from this" are claims people choose because they know they are true.

Individual Process (5 minutes): On a journal page, note recovery claims you know are true about you that could help restore the size of your ego when it is deflating.

Circle your best prospects.

Look back at the negative statements on your slips of paper. Chose the recovery claim that works best as a response to them. Use that claim in the future when you need it.

If you are working with a partner or group, share the recovery claim you will use in the future.

Erin was coming from a summer school class when I saw her. "How are you doing? Are you continuing to be an apprentice of the Woo Master?" "Sure am," she said. "In fact, I just got slammed by a professor who criticized me for not having read all the books for the course. Today was the first day of class, but he said that I had the earlier part of the summer to read them. After his attack, I repeated 'I'm a good person' to myself, so his words didn't affect me. He's got the problem, not me." Erin learned to use her recovery claim as part of the repertoire of her everyday choices so her ego maintains a decent size.

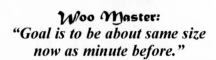

Woo Master:
***"Goal is to be about same size
now as minute before."***

People often assault themselves with their own criticisms. "I'm not interesting." "I'm not smart enough." "I'm too short." These kinds of statements have the same consequence for our egos as derogatory comments from others. Attacked by our own self-accusations, our egos shrink, so we lose our balance and our ability to be happy and effective. When we hear one of these criticisms, we can use a recovery claim to prevent ego deflation. Adding a "but" to an accusation can also make a big difference.

When an accusation arises within us, we just add "but" and then contest the criticism. For example, to the accusation "I think I'm not interesting," we might add, "but I know I'm a good person." "I'm not smart enough" could become "I'm not as smart as I wish, but I'm smart enough." "I'm too short" shifts to "I'm short, but tall enough." "But" allows us to set our inner critic straight, so our egos maintain a good size.

The point of recovery claims is to keep our egos large enough so we can feel good enough to create the lives we want. On the one hand, they add an option to the way we react to others. We cannot control what people say and do to us, but we can control our response to what they say and do. On the other hand, they give us some influence over our inner critic, so we put a stop to the negative judgments we make about ourselves.

If we think it, we can change it.

With respect to balance, becoming too ego inflated can also get us into trouble. When it happens to a person in authority, it can have damaging consequences for an organization. The extremes of "too little" and "too big" can both have undesirable consequences. In contrast, when we balance "too little" and "too big," we create an ego size that is "just right."

By realizing that "just right" (not too big or too little) is the real size of human beings, we bring under control our tendency to always compensate for feelings of inadequacy. Knowing our real size, we can stop experiencing our feelings of inadequacy as signs of a personal defect and embrace them as a part of our dual nature. With this more balanced sense of self, we are less concerned about always managing our ego size because we have discovered the folly of it.

Woo Master:
"When we know real size is not too big and not too little,
who can touch us with harsh words?
We say, 'Yes, I am this'. 'Yes, I am that'.
Then laugh. Not foolish, just wooish."

Increasing Autonomy And Authenticity

To develop more autonomy and authenticity, learning to embrace the opposites is essential. To achieve this, we must learn to accept the possibility of what we fear: Looking bad and rejection, being dependent and not having control, being wrong, and feeling insecure. When we accept rejection and embrace acceptance, for example, our capacity for balance increases. The opposites become viable choices, so there is less fear and greater well-being. Accepting what we fear becomes a path of liberation.

Individual Process (25 minutes): What are you willing to accept that you have been fearing? Create statements that include the opposites, such as "I want to be accepted, but I can accept rejection." When you have finished your statements, write a brief letter to yourself explaining how you will now live more fully as the person that you are.

If you are working with a partner or group, read your letters.

We establish more autonomy by declaring our ability to go one way or the other between the opposites. Accepting the two possibilities gives us greater flexibility in our response to what people say or do to us. Someone says, "Boy, you're looking awful today." "Yes, I can really look awful. But, who says looking awful isn't part of my freedom?"

To the extent that we embrace the opposites within us, we make it harder for others to reach into our hearts and crush us. "You're pretty insecure." "Yes, I'm insecure at times, but that's okay. I love the neediness of it. Just imagine what I'm getting from your concern." When we quit resisting and accept what we automatically fear, we can begin to play with our dual nature and with others. Then, the smile of the Woo Master emerges from within us.

Woo Master:
"Accepting being ordinary is extraordinary."

Part II

Everyone Is Telling Stories

Most of us are unaware of how often we make up stories. Some stories, like lies, we create to protect ourselves. We also tell stories about what we will do without the least intention of doing it. We fabricate stories about situations that we do not fully understand because we need the certainty of knowing. We weave stories about the past, present, and future that become torturous thought prisons. When we understand how telling stories can ruin our reputation, relationships, and sense of well-being, we can make new choices and change what we do. Personal power is expanded by gaining access to new choices. Practice is living a choice into use.

Chapter 8

Weaving Stories
Of Deception

Humans are fiction writers. We create stories to deceive others so we can manage the size of our egos. We omit facts to impress them, or resort to lying for self protection. When we lie, we twist or falsify the facts, while deception by omission is the suppression of information that makes us look bad. By omitting certain facts about ourselves, we fail to tell the whole story. We may turn in a beautifully designed project at work, but not mention that we worked day and night for weeks to create it. If others knew, they might not think we are as brilliant as we want to appear. We may also hold back certain opinions for fear that they will be unpopular.

Woo Master:
*"Would we deceive others,
if life were only weekend long?"*

Individual Process (20 minutes): In your journal, record the ways you deceive by omission. What information do you withhold so you are seen in the best possible light?

Perhaps you conceal facts in order to look good or establish control. Be aware of what you exclude from your stories so you can shine in other peoples' eyes.

Note how concealing information helps you look good and achieve acceptance, establish independence and gain control, be right, or achieve security.

Briefly describe the lies you have told or tell regularly. Include blatant lies where you gave false information to protect yourself or twisted the facts to gain an advantage.

Note how those lies helped you look good and attain acceptance, maintain independence and control, be right, or attain security.

Recess of the mind: Take a few minutes to close your eyes and reflect on your discoveries about deception by omission and lying. Are there choices you would like to make?

If you are working with a partner or group, share what you learned.

Do you know someone who lies consistently but has lost awareness of it? At times, lying becomes so automatic that we deceive ourselves. We lie and cleverly fool ourselves into thinking that we are being honest. Some people, whose ideals are not lofty, may choose to lie and then lead lives full of cunning deceptions.

> *We can become so embedded in deception that we no longer know what the truth is.*

We Pay A Price For Deception

When we deceive, especially when it is an outright lie, we diminish our good standing in the eyes of others. They may know we have lied, but not tell us. Without understanding why, our relationships and reputation are undermined.

Marta signed the attendance roll and then snuck out of class. She hoped that I would not notice her deception, but I did. She was a good-hearted young woman, but her lie caused me to mistrust and think less of her. In what must have seemed an inconsequential act on her part, she destroyed trust, the most precious thing in a relationship. In an instant, she damaged our relationship and lost her good reputation. What a huge cost for one moment of indiscretion. How often do we do this?

> *Those we deceive may know or suspect*
> *that we have lied, but not tell us.*
> *Those who do we may dislike*
> *for being "brutally honest."*

Another problem with deception is that it creates a fear of being found out. This fear can reduce self-esteem, lower confidence, and make us uncomfortable around those we deceive. The more we tell the truth, the less fear we carry. As a result, we feel better about ourselves, more confident in our actions, and more comfortable with others.

Individual Process (15 minutes): In your journal, briefly describe the last time someone deceived you. How did it make you feel? How did you feel about the person? What did the deception do to the relationship?

If you are working with a partner or group, share your experience.

When people try to deceive us, they destroy our trust, which is essential for creating good relationships with our mates, children, friends, or co-workers. Once trust is damaged, it is extremely difficult to repair, as people who are caught in romantic affairs discover. In contrast, people who nurture trust are likely to have relationships that work well.

Woo Master:
"Loss of trust is like loss of hair on
balding man. Both difficult to grow again."

Honesty Is A Choice

Deception is so automatic, we fall into it without noticing. When we catch ourselves in a lie, we may be unwilling to tell the truth because we are afraid of looking bad. I struggled with this issue after telling a lie.

I play squash, which is an indoor racquet sport. Matt is one of the great players at my club. He had arranged for a professional to come to give squash lessons. When he told me about it, I promised that I would sign up for a lesson. When the time for the lessons approached, I was busy, so I failed to keep my promise. Also, I had heard a rumor that all the lesson times had been filled, although I made no effort to confirm it.

The date for the lessons passed and I saw Matt at the club. He confronted me: "I thought you were going to sign up for a lesson? We didn't have enough people and the teacher was disappointed. I don't know if he'll come again." In response, I lied. "I'm sorry, I called the front desk and someone told me that all the lesson times had been filled." (Notice how my lie makes someone else wrong so I can protect myself.) Matt said something more gracious than I deserved and we parted.

While Matt went for his workout, I asked myself why I had lied. I valued my relationship with him and felt that I had damaged it. Did I have the courage to tell the truth and risk looking bad? Feeling vulnerable, I found him in the weight room. "I need to tell you the truth. My relationship with you is too important to ruin it with dishonesty. I didn't call the club to find out about the lessons. I didn't sign up because I was too busy. I don't want anything but trust in our relationship, so that's why I'm giving it to you straight."

Matt had a surprised expression on his face. "You know, I haven't had anyone say that to me in a long time. Thanks." We shook hands. Since then, Matt and I have become closer. He knows he can trust what I say and, if I lie without thinking, that I will tell him.

When we successfully establish our recovery claims ("I'm good enough" or "I'm a good person"), we can reduce our deceptions. Since deception is often compensation for feeling small, the claim makes us feel big enough so we do not have to resort to lies or omissions to protect ourselves.

If we accept the possibility of looking bad, we no longer need to deceive others to look good in their eyes. If we accept being wrong, we can quit twisting the facts to insure being right. When we are able to accept what we normally avoid, we create opportunities for speaking the truth.

Individual Process (20 minutes): We have identified four

experiences people fear and avoid: Looking bad and rejection, losing independence and control, being wrong, and
insecurity.

Among these issues, which would most likely lead you to
conceal information or lie? Note those on a journal page.

In each case, briefly describe how accepting what you avoid
will allow you to be more honest. (For example, when we
accept feeling insecure, we are able to communicate our
insecurities openly instead of hiding them.)

More aware of your opportunities for honesty, note what
you want to change to reduce your deceptions. Are there forms
of deception you would like to keep?

If you are working with a partner or group, share your decisions.

After doing this work, most people want to reduce their
deceptions when they are trying to protect themselves. They
often maintain the choice to lie when someone could be hurt
by the truth. (They would avoid responding to the question
"Do you like my new hair style?" with "I don't like it much
because it doesn't suit you.")

Soon after completing this work, Cindy called me because
she had missed class. She said her car was stuck in the snow.
I thanked her for telling me, said "Goodbye" and hung up.
In a few minutes, the phone rang again. It was Cindy. "I'm
sorry but I just lied to you. The truth is that I didn't feel like
coming to class and that was the reason I wasn't there." By
admitting her lie and then telling the truth, she strengthened
her personal integrity while affirming the importance of
trust in our relationship. From this experience, she learned
how she lied without thinking and that honesty was her con-

scious choice to live another way.

Woo Master:
*"Are you someone you would want
to spend time with?"*

Chapter 9

The Power Of Your Word

Integrity emerges when our actions conform to our words. We know we are living with integrity when we say "I love you" to someone, and then demonstrate that love by helping, expressing appreciation, and showing affection. When our words and action are aligned in this way, we have created a powerful word that others can trust. Do you know people who have cultivated that kind of integrity? How well do their lives work? In contrast, whose word do you mistrust because they say one thing and do another? Are their lives effective?

Listen to what people say, but also watch what they do.

How often do we make promises without any intention of keeping them? For example, we meet a friend while taking a walk and, upon leaving, say: "I'll give you a call next week" and then fail to keep our word. This is part of the acceptable banter of our conversations. Yet, such a little thing can mean a lot to the person we promised to call. As we explore the issue of integrity, notice whether your word can be trusted. Do you say one thing and do another?

Individual Process (30 minutes): Remember times when

other people's actions did not align with their words. It could be as crucial as someone saying "I love you," who then failed to treat you in a loving way. Maybe it was as insignificant as a friend promising to stop by in the evening for a visit, then failing to appear. Perhaps you know someone who makes commitments to meet you at a definite time, yet always appears twenty minutes late. How do you feel about people who fail to keep their word? Close your eyes and reflect on these questions.

Divide a journal page in half. On one half, record examples when your word and action were aligned. On the other half, note instances when they were not aligned.

Put an X on the continuum that reflects how powerful your word is generally. When you say you are going to do something, how often do you do it?

1	2	3	4	5	6	7	8	9	10

not aligned   aligned
(seldom do what I say)   (keep my word)

Given your judgment, note how the relative power of your word affects the level of trust others feel toward you.

If you can keep promises you make to others, can you also keep promises you make to yourself?

If you have a powerful word, do you also have the capacity to say "No" so you can keep your commitments balanced?

Describe new choices you want to make.

What new practice will you try?

If you are working with a partner or group, share your discoveries.

I met Sara a decade after she did this work on integrity. She was eager to share the difference it had made in her life. "When I started keeping my promises, people could trust my word, so they began to rely on me. As a result, all aspects of my life improved. I was given more responsibility at work and my social relationships improved. People really appreciated the fact that they could depend on my word. What a difference having a powerful word has made in my life, and it's so simple."

Woo Master:
"Have powerful word, create powerful life.
Word is trusted. People listen.
When word is weak, no one listens.
You become like penny on sidewalk no one values."

Chapter 10

Just The Facts

*W*hen the facts of a situation are unclear, our imagination takes over. It creates stories about every conceivable situation, including peoples' motives. Needing an explanation, we believe the stories are true. However fanciful a story may be, it seems better than the simple facts of the case. This reaction is so automatic most of us are unaware of how much we create stories and how they affect our thoughts, our emotions, behavior, and relationships. These fictional accounts can make us happy or miserable, depending on their content.

Stories Are Automatic

When we are unclear about the facts, a story arises naturally. For example, a friend promised to meet us for lunch, then failed to appear. What stories will we tell? How will those stories affect our thoughts and emotions? "Must have forgotten" would probably not upset us too much, if loss of memory is an acceptable excuse. "Must not think much of me" might upset us because the story is about neglect and rejection. "Must be irresponsible" makes our friend wrong.

Individual Process (15 minutes): A few other scenarios follow. Imagine yourself in the situation, then write your first, instinctive response to it.

■ You have not heard from a friend, parent, child, sister, or brother for a very long time. What is the story you will make up about that? What feelings arise within you?

■ Someone you know seems to be avoiding contact with you. What is the story you will make up about that? What feelings arise within you because of that story?

■ Your boss asks you to stop by at the end of the day. What story will you make up about that? What feelings arise within you because of that?

If you are working with a partner or group, share your stories with each other.

What these stories have in common is that they are guesses about reality. Yet, we experience and respond to the guesses as if they were reality. The "boss wants to see me" can produce fearful stories, depending on the state of the organization. If things are good, we might weave a story about a promotion. If they are bad, we could ruin a whole day worrying about a layoff or a reprimand. Stories can raise us to emotional heights or lower us into dark depressions. This emotional roller coaster ride occurs because we become trapped in the stories we involuntarily tell ourselves. We believe the stories rather than questioning their validity.

For one day, be aware of how often you make up negative stories about situations or other peoples' motives. Notice how that type of story telling creates a soap opera life. Those stories give the mind something to do, but they can also create dark moods and enmity. On another day, catch yourself telling stories about your life or other people. What do you notice? What happens to the soap opera quality of your life? Can you get out of automatic and into choice about this?

Woo Master:
*"Soap operas nice to watch.
Not so nice to live in."*

"Just the facts" is a reminder that we can just state the facts and quit telling stories. We can allow our minds to live in doubt and simply face the facts. What were the facts that we received in each scenario? "My friend hasn't written and I don't know why." "I suspect he's avoiding contact with me and I don't know why." "My boss wants to see me at the end of the day and I don't know why."

By understanding how we make up stories, we can consciously seek more information. We could ask the boss who wants to see us: "What do you want to speak to me about?" Once we admit that we do not know the truth, we can seek the facts rather than spending the day in anxiety.

Individual Process (20 minutes): Briefly describe a negative story you told yourself about your life or someone else's motives, and then believed. What were your emotional reactions to the story?

Once you have the story written, state the facts you are sure about. If it is a story you have imagined about someone's motives, note how you could approach that person to get the facts.

How will you practice "Just the facts?"

If you are working with a partner or group, share what you learned.

Woo Master:
"Sometimes sunny, sometimes dark and cloudy.
Same with mind. Cannot control nature,
but can control mental weather.
When frown comes, feel smile growing."

Stopping Other People's Stories

We can supply facts to others so they do not suffer unnecessarily from their negative stories. If we forget to call someone, we can immediately tell them why. The truth works best. "I just forgot," if that is the truth. If we like the person, we might add: "I'm not happy I forgot because you're a person I value."

Individual Process (5 minutes): Think about an instance in your life where you can supply more facts to clarify a situation for someone. What facts do they need? How will you tell them?

If you are working with a partner or group, share your insights and what you will do.

Negative Stories We Tell About Ourselves

Sharon tortured herself with her own thinking, constantly undermining her confidence with self-accusations. "I would go out with friends and spend all my time conjuring up stories about what they were saying about me behind my back or what they were thinking about me. These were always negative stories so I constantly felt terrible about myself and awkward in their presence. Once I understood this, it was easier than I expected to quit telling myself those stories. By stopping the stories, I immediately began to feel better about myself. I also began to enjoy being with my friends."

Sharon became aware of other damaging stories she was telling herself. One story was "I'm not likeable." When she realized that was merely another story, she put a stop to it. "I don't need to make up that story. All I have to do is be me. It's up to others to decide whether they like the me I am. When I started to honestly share myself with others, I noticed that, not only did they like me, but I liked me."

When we relax and express who we are,
we attract people who like that.
So, what is the point of pretending?
It just attracts the wrong people.

Individual Process (15 minutes): In your journal, identify negative stories you tell yourself about yourself as brief newspaper headlines. (For example, "Most boring person alive.")

Once you have recorded the headlines, take a story that diminishes your sense of well-being and write a paragraph about how your life will change when you stop telling yourself that story.

What new headline would you write?

Recess of the mind: Close your eyes and reflect on what you learned.

If you are working with a partner or group, share your discoveries.

"I don't know" is one of the most helpful statements we can make. It can quickly stop the stories that make us miserable. We keep thinking we know, when, in fact, we do not. We cannot read peoples' minds, so we cannot know their motives. We constantly make up stories about situations that are later proven wrong. When we live in the story "I'm not an interesting person," we become less interesting because we reduce our contact with others. We then fail to communicate enough about ourselves to become interesting to them. These stories cause us to suffer because we believe they are true. When we begin to question their truth and admit "I don't know," new options for living appear.

Woo Master:
"'I don't know' is quick way
to pull plug on soap opera life."

Chapter 11

Stories Can Become Thought Prisons

Many of us live in negative stories about the past, present, and future that make us feel trapped and miserable. We are generally unaware that these stories have a detrimental effect on us. Having lived in these thought prisons for so many years, we no longer see the bars, so we are blind to what is controlling and tormenting us. Once we discover how our stories trap us, we gain greater access to choice and the freedom to change our thinking and our lives.

Stories About The Past

Keith entered my office excited to share something with me. I had just finished reading his journal, where he repeatedly blamed his father for a host of his problems. I wanted to talk to him about it. Before I could begin, he said: "Last night I had a huge realization. It was never my father! It was me! All these years I've been blaming him for my life not working, but I'm the one who's failed to make it work. I have felt so hopeless about changing my life until this moment. Now that I know I did it, I can change it."

Difficult, even terrible, things happen to people. Stories

about these experiences can become thought prisons that trap us in the past and diminish our power to change. Many of us carry at least one story. It might be: "When I was young, my parents divorced and my dad left. I felt abandoned by him. Because of that, I can't trust men. Unable to trust, I go from one man to another." Another person, adopted as a child, might live in the story: "I don't know who I am because I don't know who my biological parents are." Without diminishing the fact that these experiences occurred, is it possible to stop the effects of the stories and create the lives we want?

Individual Process (20 minutes): On a journal page, write the leading story you tell about your past that may be stopping you from living the life you want now.

Describe how the story is limiting your thinking and life options.

Consider the choices that emerge when you stop telling the story. Describe changes you could make.

If you are working with a partner or group, discuss how your story has been limiting you and what changes you would like to make.

By giving up our stories about the past, we declare that our lives are beginning now.

When we take responsibility for our lives, an opportunity for change appears. The woman who blamed her father for her problem with men could admit: "What happened with my father was traumatic, but I don't have to let it dominate and ruin the rest of my life. I can change how I relate to men." When we live in the story of the past, we remain trapped there, thinking we cannot undo what the past has done to us. When we abandon the story, we can take action, experiment, and change.

Woo Master:
"When I trip on root, I have choice.
I can lie on ground and blame root
or pick myself up and go on my way."

Stories About The Present

Tragedies can be blessings; blessings can become tragedies. A friend of mine was emotionally devastated by the loss of a woman's love. I held him in my arms while he cried. Overcome with grief, talking did not help. I knew it would be a long recovery. At that moment, he was convinced that it was a great tragedy. In time, he healed and met another woman, who is now his wife. She combines an impressive intelligence with a kind heart and a wonderful lightness of being. He could not have found a more wonderful mate. "Soul mates" is the thought that comes to mind when I think about them. So, was his earlier loss a tragedy or a blessing?

The mind continuously sorts experiences into "good" and "bad." It snaps into judgment about each experience without seeing the bigger picture: "How tragic that I'm being laid off!" Yet, looking back on our lives, we see that sometimes a tragedy, like losing a job, turned into a blessing. Sometimes what seemed a blessing turned sour. Realizing this, judgments made about situations in our lives can be suspended by asking two questions: "Can what I believe to be tragic turn into a blessing over the long run?" "How do

I know that what seems like a blessing won't turn bad?" There is an interesting story from Taoism that illustrates this broader perspective.

An old man lived in a small village. The kings were jealous of him because he possessed a magnificent white horse. They wanted to buy the horse, but the old man refused to sell it. One morning, the old man discovered the horse was gone. People in the village thought this was a great misfortune and they scolded him for failing to sell the horse. The old man replied: "Don't go too far—simply say that the horse is not in the stable. This is the fact; everything else is a judgment. Whether it is a misfortune or not, how do you know?" However, the people were convinced that a treasure had been lost and that it was a misfortune.

Two weeks later, the horse reappeared. It had not been stolen, but had fled into the wilderness. With the horse were a dozen wild horses. Hearing the news, the people told the old man that he was right and they were wrong. The horse's disappearance was a blessing after all. The old man said, "Again you are going too far. Just say that the horse is back, and say that twelve horses have come with the horse—but don't judge. Who knows whether it is a blessing or not? It is only a fragment. Unless you know the whole story, how can you judge? You read one page of a book, so how can you judge the whole book? You read one sentence on a page—how can you judge the whole page? You read a single word in a sentence—how can you judge the whole sentence? And even a single word is not in the hand—life is so vast—a fragment of a word and you have judged the whole! Don't say that this is a blessing, nobody knows. I am happy in my no-judgment; don't disturb me."

Because they had been wrong before, the people remained silent. Yet, they were thinking that good fortune had fallen on the old man.

The old man had a son, who began to break the wild horses. A week later, he fell from one of them and broke both his legs. The people gathered as before. They told the old man that he had been right. What seemed to be good fortune was misfortune in disguise. The old man replied: "You are obsessed with judgment. Say only that my son has broken his legs. Who knows whether this is a misfortune or a blessing? Nobody knows. Again a fragment, and more is never given to you. Life comes in fragments, and judgment is about the total."

Soon afterwards, the country went to war and all the young men in the village were forced into military service. Only the old man's son was left behind because he was disabled from his serious fall. The people gathered, crying and weeping because their sons had been taken from them. They told the old man that he was right, his son's accident had been a blessing. "Only say this," replied the old man, "that your sons have been forced to enter the military and my son has not been forced. But nobody knows whether it is a blessing or a misfortune. Only God knows."

The old man lived with awareness of "maybe." In the larger picture of life, what seems a misfortune may not be. What appears as a windfall may prove otherwise. We cannot know. Yet, most of us take a simple fact and create a story about it, making it into a disaster or windfall. The disaster story will send us into frustration or depression. The windfall story will make us feel great. In either case, the story is a thought prison of our own making.

Individual Process (15 minutes): Looking back on your life, recall an example of a "misfortune" that evolved into a blessing or an instance of "good fortune" that turned sour.

Now, think about the present. Are you currently in judgment about a "misfortune" or "good fortune" that could be changed into a "maybe?" What changes might occur in your thinking if you quit making judgments about "good" and "bad" and shifted to "maybe?"

If you are working with a partner or group, share what you discovered. What does it tell you about story telling and human suffering?

The mind avoids doubt and aims for certainty. It likes making the quick judgments of "good" and "bad." It dislikes "maybe." Thinking about it carefully, we find that we are uncertain about the consequences of many things that occur in our lives. "The worst thing just happened," I heard a young woman say to a friend. "Jack decided to break off our relationship. I'm crushed! I feel like my life is ruined." If we listen, we can hear the old man saying "Maybe, maybe." By admitting that we do not know, we put a stop to our torturing stories and keep our options open.

Woo Master:
*"'Don't know' keeps mind clear
and alert for action. Like bent knees
waiting for opportunity to go right or left."*

Stories About The Future

There is another kind of story we tell. It is about the future. Some people tell stories about the future that make them feel good. Others invent stories that make them pessimistic and cynical. A woman came to see me who wanted to add my course. Although many others were ahead of her on a wait list, I added her when I heard her reason for wanting to do the work. "I always think the worst about the future. If I'm in a relationship, I'm sure it won't last. If I think of my future, I'm convinced it won't work. When I think of marriage, I'm certain it will end in divorce. My future is always gloomy."

Inventing a story about a bright future will make people more optimistic about their life chances, so it is understandable why they do it. But why would someone develop a story about the future that is negative and causes suffering? They may want to avoid the disappointment and pain of unrealized expectations. Afraid their hopes for the future will be dashed, they stop developing positive expectations and shift to negative ones instead. If they expect the worst and it occurs, they can say: "Just as I thought." When it turns out right, they can be surprised. "What a stroke of luck!" Of course, the initial joy of good luck may be followed by the thought: "I'll bet it won't last." Secretly, they are probably hoping it will.

The human mind is fascinating. It tells us a gloomy story about the future to prevent disappointment, yet the story makes us miserable while we wait for the result. The Woo Master would say "Cannot foretell future, so do not know" when asked what the future has in store, but that is not as much fun as telling a story about it. Even when the story makes us miserable, it seems preferable to the simple fact: "I really don't know what will happen."

Individual Process (20 minutes): In your journal, describe the story you tell yourself about your future. Once you have finished, underline the positive and negative predictions with two different colored pens. Add up the number of positive and negative statements, so you can see the emphasis of your story. Then, think about how you developed the ability to foretell the future. What makes you believe it will turn out that way?

If you are working with a partner or group, share your stories about the future and what you learned from them.

Negative stories about the future are similar to the thought prisons we occupy about the past and present. They make us feel trapped. Resigned to our fate, we quit taking action, or do so halfheartedly. One day, I asked Nancy what she saw in her future. "I don't see a man I'll have a permanent relationship with, that's for sure," she said without hesitating. "What if you gave up that story?" was my next question. "Well, I guess I might begin to look more seriously again." When we stop telling our stories and embrace the idea that we do not know, we can give up our resignation and try to create what we need.

Woo Master:
"Only by moving my feet do I have chance of reaching mountain top."

Most of us cannot help telling a story about the future. We resist admitting that we do not know. If we are unable to tolerate the doubt, then our lives work better if we create a positive story, since the choice is arbitrary anyway. Beth changed her life with this realization.

On the first day of class, I noticed a young woman dressed in dark clothing sitting as far from the other students as possible. I could tell that she felt uncomfortable. Each day she appeared in drab colors and sat alone. Checking the roll, I learned her name was Beth. One day, I asked her how she was feeling about the work we had been doing. She said she was doing fine and was learning a lot. Concerned about her, this response reassured me.

As part of their work at that time, students spent four to eight hours in isolation going carefully through their lives from their earliest memory. They examined the pattern of their lives and how their choices influenced its development. With the weekend approaching, the time had come for the isolation experience.

When the class met again the next week, I hardly recognized Beth. She was dressed in bright colors and she was talking to others and smiling. I watched her for a few minutes, thinking to myself "Beth has changed." At the beginning of class, I routinely ask if anyone wants to share. On this day, I looked at Beth and smiled. "Okay," I said, "do you want to tell us what happened?" With enthusiasm, she started her story.

She told us that she had spent several hours examining how her life had developed and the choices she had made that were turning points. "Suddenly, I remembered an early experience when I made a huge decision. Something happened that was a very big disappointment to me. When it occurred, I made a decision to quit expecting good things to happen and, instead, to take a negative view. That way, I wouldn't have to experience the pain of disappointment again. Then it hit me! My decision was just an arbitrary choice and I could make a different decision. So, I decided to quit thinking negatively and develop a positive outlook. I've changed who I'm choosing to be. I feel transformed."

By changing her thinking, Beth had transformed herself. No longer withdrawn, she became a part of the group and took an active role in discussions. By the end of the term, she was planning her future with confidence and optimism.

Part III

Making Relationships Work

Woo Master:
"Good gardeners know 'healthy root, healthy plant'.
Same with relationships.
Healthy trust, healthy relationship."

*W*e are about to deeply explore how psychological type affects our relationships. The following overview of Carl Jung's ideas about type will be helpful if you are unfamiliar with his theory or you would welcome a review. To receive the full benefit of the following two chapters, please complete the type test in the opening pages of *Please Understand Me II* by David Keirsey or *Please Understand Me* by David Keirsey and Marilyn Bates. Read about your type in the appropriate places in either book. If you have internet access, the test can be completed and you can learn about your type at [http://Keirsey.com/]. Another option is to find someone in your community who is certified to administer the Myers-Briggs Personality Inventory.

Jung's thinking about psychological types arose from his conflicts with Sigmund Freud. He observed that Freud was extroverted while he was introverted. There were also other differences that made their relationship difficult. Jung wondered why. A question occurred to him: "Are we born into a psychological type that establishes an operating mode for our lives?" After years of research, his answer was "Yes."

Eventually, he would identify as types extrovert and introvert, sensation and intuition, thinking and feeling. While these attributes appear in combination to produce a unique personality, Jung argued that they exist in each person. Some will be dominant at the conscious level while the rest remain in the unconscious to be developed. Jung called the conscious types "superior functions," while he referred to their unconscious counterparts as "inferior functions." When situations allow us to use our superior qualities, we feel confident and secure. If circumstances force us to rely on our inferior side, we will feel awkward and insecure. Introverts experience this insecurity when called upon to give a public speech. Extroverts sometimes feel awkward in silence.

Although Jung believed that psychological types were biologically inherited, he argued that changes of personality were possible by consciously developing our inferior qualities. This is why he discussed psychological types in relationship to "individuation," the process of becoming a more integrated person.

Since the intricacies of psychological type are explained in *Please Understand Me II* and *Please Understand Me*, the types are only briefly described here.

■ Introvert and Extrovert

These types have different orientations to the social world.

Introverts prefer solitude. When required to interact socially, they tend to evaluate and monitor their thoughts before
speaking. Extroverts love company and tend to speak spontaneously, sometimes judging what they say afterwards.
Stated simply, introverts cannot help being quiet and extroverts cannot help talking. Introverts feel more comfortable
and gain energy when they are alone. They feel awkward
and lose energy when they have to interact. Extroverts feel
more comfortable when they are with others. They gain
energy through interaction.

As opposites, introverts and extroverts are strongly attracted to each other. While this is an opportunity to achieve
wholeness in a relationship, it is also a major cause of conflict because opposite types try to change each other.

■ **Sensation and Intuition**

There are fundamental differences in the way people perceive the world. Intuitive types develop an orientation to
the world by trusting their inner hunches. They have a
sweeping, impressionistic view of life. In contrast, sensation types perceive the world using their five senses. They
are careful observers. If these two types entered a room
together, they would experience it differently. The intuitive
type would have a difficult time describing the contents and
details of the room afterwards, but would have a good grasp
of the room's general character. The sensation type could
provide a more detailed description of the room's contents,
including its colors.

These types tend to annoy each other. Intuitive types may
scarcely be aware of the mess they make. Sensation types,
who will notice anything out of place, will experience the
intuitive person's mess as a dump site. A conflict might

develop over this, with sensation types thinking the intuitive person is experiencing the mess the way they do. The intuitive person will wonder why there is a problem since the mess is hardly noticed. As opposites, intuitive and sensation types may try to change each other and be frustrated by their lack of success.

■ Thinking and Feeling

"Thinking" and "feeling" are different ways people make decisions. While often guided by their values, thinking types rely on objectivity and logic when they make decisions. They carefully weigh their choices to make sure that they select the best option. When making decisions, feeling types are more inclined to be subjective, relying on their personal values more than logic. They are more inclined to seek the "right" choice, rather than the objectively "best" one.

"Feeling" does not mean "emotional." Like thinking types, feeling types are usually careful evaluators of their options. Depending on the circumstances, both types can become irritable, moody, or angry.

Thinking and feeling types are likely to have conflicts over decision-making. Thinking types may believe their feeling counterparts are too irrational. Feeling types can become annoyed at the cold calculation of a thinking person. Since most people fail to understand that the conflict arises from differences of type, they may conclude that the other person has a defect of character. Usually, this will initiate reform efforts, which adds conflict to the relationship.

■ Judging and Perceiving

"Judging" and "perceiving" focus on peoples' preference for planning or spontaneity. Judging types love order and planning. They are likely to have a well-developed list of tasks to accomplish each day. When vacation time comes, they will want to plan well ahead of the trip because they enjoy it. In contrast, perceiving types usually avoid planning, because they thrive on spontaneity. They can enjoy a degree of disorder because it allows them to create in the face of shifting circumstances. A minimum of planning is their preference before an impending vacation. They welcome the excitement of the unknown.

When these types are in a relationship, they tend to irritate each other. Judging types will be conscientious, planning each day so their goals can be reached. They are gratified by their daily achievements. Perceiving counterparts tend to achieve results following a more free-flowing process, often without clear plans. They like to keep their options open. A judging type will think the perceiving type is disorganized and irresponsible. A perceiving type will think the judging person is too driven and rigid. If they are mated, they may have problems over the management of money. If they are co-workers on a project, they are likely to experience conflicts over planning and issues of responsibility.

In addition to expanding our awareness of psychological types, we will explore other important relationship issues: Attraction, ideals, communication, problem-solving, and how to clean up relationship issues from the past.

Chapter 12

Quiet And Talkative People

Zoos are fascinating. Some animals are quiet and shy while others are noisy, outgoing, and aggressive. Some are playful. Others are more serious and reserved. We could be describing the animals in our human zoo. What are our biologically inherited tendencies and temperaments and how do they lead us to act in predictable, instinctual ways? By answering this question, we will learn that our psychological type influences us at a deeper level than we know. This awareness is crucial for understanding ourselves and our patterns of conflict and cooperation with others.

Given our society's emphasis on competition and social graces, extroverts have clear advantages because they are rewarded for expressing their natural tendency to be social. Introverts must make an effort to be social, since it goes against their nature. If they hold back, preferring to be alone, they may be labeled "backward" or "antisocial." Parents may feel there is something wrong with a quiet child. When they do, this may be expressed directly as criticism or indirectly in words of encouragement to join social groups or to speak up. Affected by this judgment, introverts may struggle to overcome self-doubts and loss of confidence, feeling the pressure to prove their worth each day. Unaware of their psychological type, they may not fully understand why they suffer.

In contrast, extroverts may suffer when they cannot control their impulse to talk. One very talkative woman put it as a question: "Why can't I just shut up and listen?" While this question arises for a few extroverts, many seem oblivious to what introverts know so well. As one introverted woman put it: "Extroverts are so taken with themselves and their ideas, it never dawns on them that they are continuously shining the spotlight on themselves. Seldom do they shine the light on the quiet soul who is listening."

Spotlight Strategies

To avoid being in the spotlight, introverts ask questions and avoid making statements. This strategy is for self-protection because they feel awkward divulging personal information about themselves, especially to strangers. By asking questions, they keep the attention on others and away from themselves. They might welcome our attention and questions if they feel secure with us. If they are with trusted friends or family, they can even become obsessive talkers.

> *The purpose of communication is as much about self-protection and self-promotion as it is about giving or exchanging information.*

Unlike introverts, extroverts love to shine the spotlight on themselves. In a conversation with an extrovert, we may hear statements such as "What I think," "What I believe," "What happened to me recently." When their extroversion is extreme, they may scarcely listen, sometimes appearing as if they are not interested in getting to know us as long as we get to know them.

Individual Process (20 minutes): If you are introverted, note the things you do to keep the spotlight on others. If you are extroverted, what do you do to keep the spotlight on yourself? (If you are an "X" in the scoring system, select your dominant tendency.)

Briefly describe what you get from your spotlight tactics.

Note changes that you could make to create more balance between introversion and extroversion within yourself.

Close your eyes and imagine having made those changes. What do you notice?

If you are working with a partner or group, share your discoveries.

Woo Master:
"Too talkative, others quit listening.
Too quiet, others will not take you into account.
Instead of being crashing waves or silent pond,
seek balance as deep river current."

Alternative Group Process (50 minutes): If you are working in a group, consider the following as an alternative or addition to the individual process. It can also be adapted for partners.

Start by identifying the introverts and extroverts in your group. You will need at least one of each type. If there are more extroverts than introverts, arrange the group with one introvert as the nucleus and two or three extroverts. For partners, there needs to be one introvert and one extrovert.

The process employs the following rules:

■ Extroverts may only ask questions about the introvert's life and they are required to listen carefully and not make statements of their own. The goal of the extrovert is to learn as much about the introvert as possible.

■ Introverts may only make statements about themselves and they cannot ask questions. The mission of the introvert is to share deeply.

When guiding the exercise with a group, stop the interaction after five minutes and ask: "How many introverts have already asked a question? How many extroverts have made a statement about their opinions or themselves?" If people have broken the rules, have them explain why. After this period of sharing, resume the process for another ten minutes.

When the question and answer period is drawn to a close, separate the introverts and extroverts into groups facing each other. Explain that the next part of the work will be a rare opportunity to talk honestly to each other.

Begin with the question: "What most annoys you about the other type?" Start by asking for a response from an introvert. After hearing from that person, turn to the extroverted group for a volunteer. Alternate between the groups, calling on one person at a time.

Keep the group's focus on the question until it has been fully explored, then introduce the second question: "What do you most appreciate about the other type?"

After about twenty minutes, ask people to share what they learned from each other.

Woo Master:
"Lion and lamb will not
rest long together in peace.
Like some noisy and quiet people.

Opportunities For Change

When they learn to feel good about their quiet nature, introverts may be more willing to risk being in the spotlight. Extroverts, realizing they cannot help talking, might decide to practice listening. By understanding their nature, they have the option to accept it or try to change.

For some people, accepting their nature
is a major change.

Individual Process (20 minutes): Divide a journal page in half. On one half, describe what you like about being an introvert or extrovert. On the other, describe what you dislike about being your type.

How does what you like help you to accept your type?

Examining what you do not like, what changes would you like to make? Briefly describe practices you will undertake to produce those changes.

If you are working with a partner or group, share your ideas.

An Interesting Tension

There is a tension within us we can honor. It is the conflicting tendency to accept and to reject ourselves. Accepting ourselves helps us feel secure and it provides relief from the constant struggle of trying to change. Yet, in our comfort, we may hear a voice in us say: "I shouldn't be too complacent, because there are things I dislike about myself that I want to change." The tendency to accept and reject ourselves is part of the tension of being human. We cannot escape it, but can live with it as a choice.

> *Our inclination to both accept and reject ourselves*
> *sets up an inner conflict that confuses us,*
> *but helps us to evolve.*

Kiso was a young woman from Japan who experienced pressure to participate in class because of the extroverted norms of our culture. She asked me to encourage her. On occasion, I called on her to share. After completing the work above, she made a decision. "Now I realize that I'm quiet and I like it. There is something beautiful about the silence. When I accept that as my nature, I feel completely at home. So, now I want to choose to be that quiet nature. I don't want you to call on me any more, but I may participate if I feel like it."

For the rest of the term, Kiso remained quiet, although she participated fully in the small group work. I could tell that she was more comfortable during the large group sharing, because she was not criticizing herself.

The following semester Kiso appeared at my office door

with tears streaming down her face. "Something just happened that's making me miserable," she said. "My professor just spoke to me after class. He said: 'You aren't participating and I want you to know that's not acceptable. If you want a good grade in this class, you must participate!'" Kiso had said little in response to this threat, but the emotion overwhelmed her as she burst into tears while walking out of the classroom.

"What am I to do?" she asked. "I don't want to participate. I'm quiet and I like it."

"So, what will you tell the professor?" I asked.

She thought for a moment, then a smile came across her face. "I'll just say: 'I'm a person who values my quiet nature and I don't like talking'."

"What will you say if the professor says: 'You will get a lower grade'."

"I will say: 'It is a price I will pay to be myself'."

The next time she saw her professor, she told him what she had decided. She lived in harmony with her quiet nature for the rest of the semester, and she did receive a lower grade. This was a small price given the freedom she had achieved. It is the kind of freedom that emerges when we have been told we will be punished for disobedience and we decide to pay the price.

Before Kiso returned to Japan, she came to say goodbye. "I am returning to my home. Because I have accepted my quiet nature, I did not let your culture hurt me. I still feel good about myself, although there were others who tried to make me feel that there was something wrong with me.

There is nothing wrong with me." We smiled at each other, then hugged. As I watched her walk away, she turned to smile one last time. Tears were running down her cheeks and I could feel them welling up in my eyes. My tears were bowing down to her nature and to the real power of being she had attained.

Chapter 13

$\mathcal{F}$amilies $\mathcal{A}$re $\mathcal{L}$ike $\mathcal{Z}$oos

*J*magine a zoo where lions, gazelles, monkeys, hippos, and mountain goats are fenced in together. It would be an interesting part of the zoo, because a lot of conflict would take place there. Change the combination of animals and we alter the nature of their social life. For a moment, think about our families, friendships, workplaces, and church communities in this light. Each is a combination of different psychological types, which produce their own patterns of cooperation and conflict. Think about how much antagonism arises from differences of introversion and extroversion alone. The quiet person may want to stay home with a good book, while the extrovert wants to go out with friends. When you add the temperament types to this difference, the possibilities for misunderstanding mount quickly.

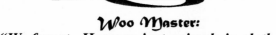

$\mathcal{W}$oo $\mathcal{M}$aster:
"We forget. Humans just animals in clothes."

The temperament types:

- Sensation Perceiving type (SP): Loves to be free. Does not want to be confined or obligated. Irresponsible.

Avoids belonging. Alive. Likes to have fun. Lives for today.

■ Sensation Judging type (SJ): Helper. Serves society. Likes being bound and obligated. Responsible. Must belong. Likes to build and lead organizations. Creates for the future.

■ Intuitive Thinking type (NT): Wants to understand, control, predict, and explain reality. Must be competent. Logical. Self-critical and often critical of others. Lives for work. Not emotionally tuned in. Somewhat aloof. Realist.

■ Intuitive Feeling type (NF): Seeks self-improvement. Always becoming and longs for meaning. Needs to be genuine (no role playing). Often shuns logic for values. Seeks relationships. Emotionally in tune with others. Dreamer.

Andy learned how differences of temperament affect relationships when he started his own business. A gifted artist, he created and imprinted his own designs on tee shirts and other clothing. His art being unique, the clothing sold well, so he hired a management staff. Working together, the company expanded rapidly, until the clothing was being sold across the country.

Andy's partners were always on time for work, intently focused on planning, and followed rigid daily routines. Andy was often late, stayed into the night creating new designs, and liked to vary his work schedule. While his partners were inclined to worry, he took things in stride. They began to pressure him to become more responsible and to worry more about the fate of the company. Their efforts produced a great deal of conflict. Facing this stress each day, the partners developed the belief that there was something wrong with Andy. They encouraged him to seek counseling, which is why he had come to see me.

Andy knew about psychological types, so I asked him to give me an idea of his psychological type and his partners' types. "Well, let's see, I know I'm an ENFP and I would say that my partners are probably both ENTJs." A dreamer, the ENFP lives for meaning, loves spontaneity and openness, and takes things as they come. The ENTJ is the planner, who values order, competence, responsibility, and likes control. The necessity of planning within an organization requires ENTJ people. They perform important roles, but so does the creative ENFP. If they are extreme cases of their type, they will have a difficult time understanding each other. Frustrations and disputes will arise.

As Andy became aware of the conflict with his partners as a clash of types, he realized that there was nothing psychologically wrong with him. But, there was something wrong with the combination of people. "I hired two very extreme ENTJs," he said, "and they have ganged up on me." Later, when I saw him again, he said, "Well, I fired them both. After all, I own the company. I hired two new people who aren't fanatical about order, so they give me some freedom and respect. Since then the conflicts have disappeared and, because we're getting along, the business is doing even better."

All of us face these situations. Sometimes we marry or give birth to contrasting types that end up annoying us. Other aggravating possibilities are bosses, co-workers, teachers, and students. Most of these people we cannot fire, but must learn to live with. We are also a type that irritates other people in the various human zoos where we live. Each of us has interesting stories to tell about how some people naturally get along and others cannot help arguing.

*We do not mean to annoy each other, but
we cannot help being the human animals we are.*

Family Conflict and Cooperation

Your nuclear family (parents, siblings, relatives who may
have lived with you) will be the focus of the work you are
about to do. Later, you may want to use the exercise to illu-
minate other relationships.

Individual Process (25 minutes): In your journal, make a
simple diagram of the members of your family. Using the
descriptions of the temperaments noted above, type each
member and include yourself as "me." If you lived with
both parents, it might look as follows:

	Mother		Father	
	(SJ)		(NT)	
Brother		Sister		Me
(NT)		(SJ)		(NF)

Draw a solid line between members of your family where a
cooperative relationship existed. Make the line darker and
thicker to show the extent of the cooperation.

Where a relationship was characterized by conflict, draw a
broken line. Make the broken lines darker and thicker to
show the intensity of the conflict.

Circle any member of your family who was the target of a
reform effort. This would be the person another member of
your family tried to change. Draw an arrow from the insti-

gator(s) of the reform to the family member who was the target, making them darker or thicker to reflect the strength of the effort.

"What belief makes us want to change others?"

When I ask this question, people are baffled, until they hear: "Which is the best animal in the human zoo?"

"My type of course" someone will call out.

"So, what belief is behind every reform project?" I ask.

"Since we're sure our type is the best, we want others to become like us. We believe we're doing them a favor."

Woo Master:
"Humans are aware enough
to struggle over which animal is best,
but not wise enough to notice their folly."

Types Love In Their Own Way

The way people express love will vary according to their psychological type. The SP may love for the pure pleasure of it. Showing concern and offering support may be the way the SJ loves. The NT might show love by offering advice and exercising control for our good. The NF may show love through caring and teaching.

For a few minutes, note in your journal how each member of your family loves, given each person's psychological type. Include how you love, because of the type you are.

What do you see?

Recess of the mind. Close your eyes for a few moments and contemplate what you learned about psychological types, family dynamics, and love.

If you are working with a partner or group, share what you learned.

It is difficult to understand or appreciate the human animals who irritate us. Our conditioned response is to resist and try to change them. Yet, we have been doing this for thousands of years without good results. Is there another way?

Types As "Nightmares"

For the parent who has a child of an opposing type, that child can become a "nightmare," offering endless frustrations and disappointments. The child may feel the same way about a nightmare parent. If you are in your child-bearing years, what follows is for your future children. It may also be for any nightmare child that you have already brought into existence. If you have grown children, it is for existing or future grandchildren. (If children are not a part of your life, work through the process with the idea of a nightmare mate, friend, co-worker, or boss.)

Individual Process (20 minutes): In your journal, describe your nightmare child or grandchild using the temperament types. What type of child or grandchild would or does make you miserable? If you are an NT, an SP child might be your nightmare. It might upset you when that child is irresponsible and undisciplined. The opposite combination might also create a nightmare, if you were an SP and had an NT child. Wanting order, that child would probably complain about your lack of organization. Would you want to add introversion or extroversion to the description of your nightmare child?

With your description completed, briefly describe how you will try to change that child or grandchild. If you are the parent or grandparent of a nightmare child, explore what specific efforts you made or are making to reform your son or daughter, your grandson or granddaughter.

Briefly describe how you must change in order to accept your nightmare child or grandchild. If you have a nightmare child you have been trying to reform, describe a new approach you will take to create greater acceptance and love in the relationship. If you have a nightmare parent, note one change you will make to improve that relationship. Be specific.

If you are working with a partner or group, share your discoveries and choices.

Amy was a mother in her thirties when she discovered that her young son was her nightmare and that she had been trying to reform him daily. This was a source of great frustration, because she was constantly resisting his nature while failing to see any results from her efforts to change him. Sharing her experience, she said: "When I looked at who my son is, I realized that he has a beautiful spirit. It's been me who has made him wrong. I haven't been able to accept him because he's so different from me. Now, I realize that my efforts to change him will fail and that the price I'm likely to pay is the loss of his love. That's just too big a price. So, I have to change. I have to learn to accept him and to love him for who he is."

Later, Amy described the change that occurred in her relationship with her son after she changed her thinking. "Now, I'm enjoying his wild and disorganized spirit instead of thinking it's a defect. I'm noticing how funny he can be."

Woo Master:
"Accepting differences is sometimes called 'love gardening'."

Chapter 14

Attraction Does Not Insure Satisfaction

Attraction is fascinating. What draws human beings to certain ideas, lifestyles, and, most mysteriously, to each other? People spend a great deal of time falling in love, breaking up, and recovering. Many eventually marry. Some divorce and begin the process over. Entire lives can be spent repeating this process in an attempt to get it right. A fair number are captivated by people who end up hurting them. Tina suffered from this problem. She was an intelligent and engaging young woman with a history of rocky relationships. "I realized," she confessed, "that I'm attracted to men who are a little bit evil or have a character defect. I'm drawn to them because I want to take care of someone. Once I'm in a relationship with one of these guys, either he physically abuses me or I take care of him because he has a drug or alcohol problem."

Woo Master:
"Smell attractive flower before picking it."

Attraction can be so strong, it overwhelms good judgment. Before we know it, we are in relationships that, upon clearer reflection, we would avoid. Developing a deeper awareness of attraction and our many needs presents an opportunity to move out of automatic and into choice about our relationships.

Individual Process (20 minutes): In this exercise, you will create the person you are most attracted to, somewhat like selecting ingredients for a new food recipe. You can think of this attraction as a romantic interest or a potential friend. Select one or the other. To create this imaginary person, chose one type from each of the following pairs, keeping attraction in mind.

(Check one): ☐ **Introvert:** Quiet type, withdrawn, likes spending time alone.

☐ **Extrovert:** Noisy type, outgoing, likes to have an active social life.

(Check one): ☐ **Intuitive:** Relies on intuition for perceiving the world and operates from a vague sense of the physical environment. Ideas person.

☐ **Sensation:** Relies on the five senses and is keenly aware of the physical environment. Facts person.

(Check one): ☐ **Thinking:** Relies on logic for making decisions. Competence and having control are important.

☐ **Feeling:** Relies on values to make decisions. Connection and community are important.

(Check one): ☐ **Judging:** Likes to plan and have things in order.

☐ **Perceiving:** Likes to be spontaneous and can function well in disorder.

Given your choices, write a brief description of the person toward whom you would feel the greatest attraction as a possible mate or friend. Be aware of psychological type as you write.

Expanding Awareness of Needs

What do you need from a mate or friend to feel satisfied? What are your most compelling needs? Do you consciously take care of your needs?

Woo Master:
"Needs are like pets.
Care for them, they care for you."

Individual Process (30 minutes): Divide a journal page into five parts. Label them as: Social (what you need from a mate or friend to feel socially connected to her or him), spiritual (what you need from a mate or friend to fully live your spirituality), physical (what your body needs from that mate or friend), self-esteem (what you need from your mate or friend to feel good about yourself), and security (what you need from your mate or friend to feel secure).

Think about what you need from a mate or friend to be contented and happy. Record those needs in each of the five realms.

When your needs are fully identified, put a star by the most important ones. Your stars might be concentrated in one realm or distributed between them. This will reveal what areas of need are most crucial for your well-being.

On a new journal page, make a large circle. Imagine that you are looking down into a bird's nest. Add some artistic detail so it looks like a nest. This is your "need nest." Inside the nest, write down the important needs you starred. When those core needs are satisfied, you will feel secure, in control, happy, and contented, like a bird snug in its nest.

When we make decisions without awareness of our core needs, we may become depressed, lose confidence in ourselves, and not know why. Karen, a young woman in her early twenties, moved to a large city to establish her independence. Although she had only one friend there, no job, and no place to live, she went. She was courageous. Before long, she became lonely and depressed. Feeling there was something wrong with her, she lost confidence.

By moving to a large city, Karen had stepped outside her need nest. Many needs that were essential for her happiness and well-being were not being satisfied, such as having close friends, a good social life, a secure job, and a loving family. There was nothing psychologically wrong with her. She was suffering from the natural consequence of not paying attention to her needs.

Had she been aware of the needs in her nest, she would have established closer ties with the one friend she had in the city before moving there. At the very least, awareness of what happens when needs are neglected might have led to a different assessment of the situation. Instead of blaming herself, she might have concluded: "I'm choosing to take myself out of my need nest, so I must anticipate consequences. Loneliness, sadness, and lower self-confidence should be expected. Any human being who steps outside the nest will experience those feelings. So, I'm not going to beat myself up. It takes courage to do what I'm doing."

Like Karen, many people inadvertently take themselves out of their need nests, suffer, and do not know why. Knowing what happens when we step outside our nests provides us with a choice. Instead of condemning ourselves, we can applaud our courage.

Human beings dislike admitting their needs because it makes them feel weak and dependent. They believe that "needy" and "independent" are contradictory and thus cannot coexist.

If you are working with a partner or group, share what you discovered about the realms where your important needs are concentrated. What does that discovery tell you about yourself? Reveal the needs in your nest. Do you have a story like Karen where you took yourself out of your nest and then suffered for it?

Evaluating Our Attractions

Once we understand our needs, we can evaluate our attractions. We can also use that awareness to deepen existing relationships.

Individual Process (20 minutes): Review the description of the person, potential mate or friend, to whom you would be most attracted. Reexamine the psychological type of that person. Close your eyes and imagine what she or he would be like. Give the person a name, if you want.

Divide a journal page in half.

On one half, record the needs in your nest this person would find it easiest to satisfy for you. Keep psychological type in mind, because it will affect that person's ability to respond to your needs.

On the other half of the page, note the needs that person would have a difficult time satisfying.

Still feeling the attraction, make a conscious choice about whether this is a person you really need.

If your answer is "No," reexamine the summary of types above. Create a combination of types that will increase the possibility that your needs will be satisfied. If you are drawn to a planning type but know that type would not respond adequately to your needs, perhaps someone who is more spontaneous would be a better choice. You might decide that you would rather have a mate or friend who is more introverted, although extroverts fascinate you.

Combining the types with your needs in mind, write a brief description of the person, noting the needs that will be met.

Recess of the mind: Take a few minutes to close your eyes and reflect on what you have learned from this work. What new choices are emerging for you?

If you are working with a partner or group, share your

thinking about relationships, attraction, and needs.

How would our relationships improve if we
thought about who could satisfy our needs, instead of
being swept away by the magnetism of attraction?

What if people could move out of automatic about attraction and make more conscious choices? Tina, who realized that she was attracted to evil or dependent men, commented: "I guess I'm pretty deluded. I take on men who abuse me so I can satisfy my need to be a reformer, then I don't get my needs satisfied. I seem to sacrifice myself in every relationship. I'm going to put a stop to that. There are other ways to help people and have my need to be a reformer met." "Ah, clarity," the Woo Master would say with a slight smile. "Intelligence in universe."

Attraction is automatic and it can get us into trouble. We are magically drawn into a relationship with our opposite type, then become frustrated by that person's inability to satisfy important needs. However, opposites can work well together if there is a mutual willingness to appreciate the differences and a desire to make the relationship work. When we learn to respect and use the differences for mutual advantage, a sense of wholeness emerges within the relationship that is unique.

If you are in a relationship with someone who does a good job of satisfying your needs, consider doing something special for that person. Set up a time and place to express your appreciation. Ask your partner or friend if you are also doing a good job of satisfying her or his needs. Take some time to discuss how you might respond more effectively to each other's needs. You could guide the person through the

process you just completed. Together, establish the importance of expressing needs openly, so the guess work is elim-
inated.

If you are in a relationship with someone who could do a
better job of satisfying your needs or you could do a better
job, consider starting a conversation about it. It might begin
with the question: "What are our needs and how could we
improve our ability to help each other satisfy them?" You
could have your partner or friend do the process above, and
then compare what you both discovered about your need
nests. This would introduce the possibility of more awareness and choice in the relationship.

Why do we hesitate to talk openly about our needs and how
we can help each other satisfy them?

Are we afraid of appearing needy and dependent?

How would our relationships improve if we admitted our
needs and then consciously helped each other satisfy them?

Chapter 15

High Ideals Can Ruin Relationships

*I*deals are thoughts about how things should be. When people have excessively high ideals, they tend to be critical of themselves and others. "Perfectionists" are people with such high ideals that they seldom hit the mark, so they suffer many disappointments and recriminations. While they can sometimes accept the foibles of others, they have a difficult time accepting their own flaws. What do people get from this perfectionism? They get a clear sense of purpose and usually increased effectiveness because they try so very hard. They also receive more than their share of suffering.

Perfectionism is the extreme form of what we all do. Our ideals shape our perceptions, judgments, and reactions to what appears in our lives. Those ideals become part of a mental template we develop for evaluating every situation. Each pattern encompasses how we expect and desire things to be. If life corresponds to our expectations and desires, we are happy. If it fails, we become frustrated, irritable, and sometimes angry. We can experience this emotional reaction when a household project takes much longer than we desired or expected or we get stuck in a traffic jam.

Woo Master:
"Cloudy days trouble mind that longs for sun."

Disappointment And Complaint

What do unrealistic expectations have to do with relationships? Everything. Research on the family shows that a sure way to ruin a new marriage is to have excessively high ideals about it. Marriage ceremonies are a good reflection of these perfectionist ideals. Read any advice column regularly and you will discover letters from various people who describe their outrage when a wedding was spoiled because something was out of place or someone's behavior was inappropriate. Striving for the perfect wedding sets up the conditions for disappointment and complaint in marriage, which cannot possibly be perfect.

Recently, I watched a family become tense and irritable because of an approaching wedding. Initially, they were operating with the idea of the "perfect wedding," so the pressures mounted. Costs escalated and a huge debt loomed as a possibility. Luckily, the mother of the bride was wise. She saw the reckless course everyone was on and she put on the brakes. She began to encourage everyone to create an "imperfect wedding," which was as inexpensive as possible and fun. Decisions were made to lower the costs and to share the burden of preparation with friends who were willing to help. People reorganized their thinking so the planning was manageable. This was an interesting alternative to the usual approach toward weddings and the wedding was a big success.

Individual Process (25 minutes): Before you start, decide whether you want your work to focus on a relationship with a mate, friend, parent, child, sibling, or co-worker.

Write a description about how you would like that relationship to be.

When your description is complete, underline all the ideals that are embedded in your writing.

Record those ideals on another page. Beside each ideal, note the complaint that is likely to arise from it when the other person fails to live up to your expectation. If you prize attentive listening and the other person violates that ideal, you may find yourself saying in a heated moment, "Why don't you ever listen?" Notice how every complaint arises from an unrealized ideal.

Recess of the mind: Take a few minutes to close your eyes and contemplate how your ideals may be influencing your relationship. What new choices appear because of that awareness?

If you are working with a partner or group, share your experiences.

Getting Half Of What You Need Is Enough

Young people who hear that they may only get half of what they need from a close relationship often protest because they want more. Although my claim is exaggerated, I respond: "It won't be that way." They hate to hear that, but they get the point.

During the romantic phase of a relationship, a couple may develop the idea that all their needs will be satisfied within the relationship. That is part of the illusion of love. In reality, some needs will be satisfied, while others will not. Even when a relationship is good, the people we are in relationships with cannot do everything for us. Some needs they will not be equipped to satisfy because of their psychological type and the character of their own needs. If not in the relationship, how else can we satisfy our needs? Are there friends who can help? Can we draw on our own resources to take care of ourselves?

Woo Master:
"Feet do not care who rubs them."

Individual Process (25 minutes): Tear up a piece of paper into eight pieces. On each piece, identify something that you would need from your mate, friend, parent, child, sibling, or co-worker. For ideas, you can reexamine your need nest.

Once you have noted your eight needs, turn the pile upside down and mix them. Keep them face down. (You can do this process alone, but it is more fun with a friend or a group. I have designed it for individual work, and then show how the process can be tailored for partners or a group.)

With your stack of needs in front of you, turn over each need, one at a time. The following process will determine which needs will be satisfied or unsatisfied in the relationship.

1st move: Turn over your first need. Accept that the person will not satisfy that need. Consider how that will make you feel and what you will do about it. Do any complaints emerge? (Options after each move: You can close your eyes to fully experience your response or record your reaction in your journal.)

2nd move: Look at your second need. You will get this need satisfied. How will it make you feel?

3rd move: Before you reveal the next need, realize that it will not be satisfied. Turn it over. Be aware of how you will feel and respond to the situation. Any complaints?

4th move: Look at your next need. It will not be satisfied. How will this make you feel and what will do about it? Will you have complaints?

5th move and 6th move: Turn over the next two needs. Both will be satisfied. Become aware of how having those needs gratified affects you.

7th move: Before you look at your next need, know that it will be satisfied. Turn it over and notice what feelings arise.

8th move: Your final need will not be met. Turn it over. Discover how you will feel when that need is not satisfied. How will you respond? Will a complaint automatically emerge?

Option for partners and group (30 minutes): If you are working with a partner, follow the same course (with your pile of needs face down). Take turns drawing a need. Follow the response pattern as outlined above, sharing with each other how you will feel when a need is satisfied or unsatisfied. Reveal any complaints that arise from failing to have a need fulfilled.

If you are working in group, go around the circle, turning over needs one at a time (following the "Yes/No" pattern), and then share your feelings and complaints. If the group is large, smaller groups or partners can be used. After all moves are made, discuss what you learned about how ideals shape the way you want your relationships to be in contrast to the way they are. Discuss how complaints arise from your ideals.

When I take people through this work, there are many outbursts. Cries of frustration and elation spontaneously arise as they have their needs fulfilled or unfulfilled. Early in the process, I ask: "How many of you have already given up on this relationship?" Many hands go up.

Woo Master:
"All cars break down.
All relationships break down.
No need to abandon. Fix."

Given the individual differences of psychological type and needs, weddings, marriages, and other relationships are imperfect from the start. That is why the process of not getting everything we need in a relationship is such a good learning experience. Although the exercise pushes us to the extreme, failing to have some of our needs gratified is probably closer to reality than the idealistic expectation that all our needs will be met. When we understand that every relationship will be flawed, we prepare ourselves to solve problems together, rather than give up on the relationship, hoping the next one will be more perfect.

If people clearly understood that relationships cannot even approach perfection, weddings could be different. Imagine a wedding where the couple has to stand in front of family and friends, who must present challenging problems for them to resolve together. Someone from the audience might say: "Together, generate a solution to the problem about how you're going to allocate household chores so neither of you becomes angry." The couple would have to come up with a plan of action about this issue. Another person might ask: "One of you has developed a hobby that has become like an affair in your life. Your partner is feeling abandoned and neglected. How will you solve this problem together?"

The wedding audience would listen and evaluate. It would approve the marriage if the couple demonstrated a willingness to co-create solutions to tough problems. Instead of starting with an idealistic expectation, the couple might say together: "This marriage will have problems. Together, we're committed to finding creative solutions for the many problems that will inevitably arise." This approach does not mean that ideals are abandoned, but their grip is relaxed so complaint does not ruin the relationship. Instead of complaint becoming a wedge between people, it becomes a signal to co-create a solution. Having ideals, but knowing life will not be that way, is part of the tension of living in Woo.

Creating Mutual Satisfaction

Starting with the idea that all relationships will fall short of our ideals, we establish the possibility that more mutual satisfaction can be created by conscious intention. Humans are naturally creative. They can fashion relationships that are mutually satisfying, even great, if they fully possess the desire to make them work. So, what awareness do we need in order to get and give more in a relationship so needs are mutually satisfied?

We avoid asking for what we need because we dislike feeling dependent or appearing needy. Instead, we engage in "magical thinking." It goes like this: "If he (she) really loved me, he (she) would know what I need." How odd that we think our mates can read our minds. Yet, we do. Instead of asking for what we need, we wait, hoping our partner becomes aware of our need and satisfies it. We become happy and feel loved when that occurs. When our partner remains unaware of a need, we are apt to become disappointed and perhaps even angry. "Why is he (she) so insensitive? He (she) doesn't really love me."

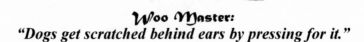

Woo Master:
"Dogs get scratched behind ears by pressing for it."

People cannot read each other's minds. Why should your partner know what you need? What if you felt completely free to ask for what you need? Try giving up the idea that being needy is a sign of weakness and that your mate, friends, parents, children, and others should be able to read your mind.

Individual Process (10 minutes): In your journal, record:

Two things you never ask for but need from your mate, friend, parent, child, sibling, or co-worker.

Two things you are afraid to ask for.

Try asking for them. See what happens.

If you are working with a partner or group, share what you discovered and what you are going to do about it.

Even when we ask for it, we will not get everything that we need. So, what do we do then? Try altering the situation. Accept the situation if it cannot be changed. Draw from ourselves to satisfy the need. Ask others for help.

Recess of the mind: Close your eyes and reflect on your relationships. Given your insights, what new possibilities do you see?

The most effective way to do the processes in the next two chapters is with a group of five people. If you are working alone, enlist four others to work with you. The process is set up for a group, but a version for partners is included. If you are working alone and cannot find four other people to work with you, seek a partner.

Chapter 16

Listening Deeply

*R*alph Ellison's *Invisible Man* reveals what happens to people when they fail to count in the eyes of the group that dominates them. While Ellison focused on the plight of African-Americans, his message is universal. It emphasizes the importance to all of us of being deeply seen and understood by others, so we know we have lived and made a difference. There is a universal human cry: "Listen to me, please. It is your listening that brings me into being!"

Effective communication is the capacity to listen and speak deeply. By learning how to communicate at that depth, we bring others and ourselves into being. Even if we are generally good listeners, we often listen on the surface. Usually, we hear the facts of the situation and the person's feelings. As we learn to listen more deeply, we develop the capacity to hear more and thus to bring more of the speaker into being.

Woo Master:
"Listening opens door to other person's mind."

Deep listening improves the quality of our relationships. We learn about the other person's struggles and point of view. We are drawn together at a deeper human level which makes us want to help each other. If we are not able to help, we can at least feel compassion. Not only are we bringing a person into being, we are bringing a good relationship into being.

Group Process (60 minutes): Working individually, take fifteen minutes to write about a situation in your life that is bothering you. It might be a transition you are going through, a problem in a relationship, or a change you are trying to make within yourself. Select an issue that is uppermost in your feelings or thinking. Write about it in some detail.

We are going to practice listening at four levels.

■ First level: Listen for the facts of the situation.

■ Second level: Listen for the person's feelings.

■ Third level: Listen for the person's needs.

■ Fourth level: Listen for the outcomes the person desires. What changes does the person want to see in the situation? These changes are not always spoken, but they can be heard "between the lines."

If you are working with a partner, see the process for two on the next page. If you are working in a group smaller or larger than five, decide beforehand how you will organize people's assignments during the process. If your group is larger than five, you can have more than one person listening from the same level during the rotations. If it is smaller than five, you can have people listen at more than one level.

In a group of five people, each will have an opportunity to be the storyteller and to listen from each of the four levels. Begin by putting the group into a circle. Assign the letters "A" through "E" in sequence around the circle. "A" will be the first storyteller. Have writing materials in hand for jotting down notes about what you are hearing.

To begin, introduce the ground rules for the process.

■ When the storyteller is talking, the listeners may not share their own experiences. They are just the receivers of the communication, and nothing more.

■ The point of the exercise is to listen to each person tell his or her story. It is not about fixing the problem, so avoid giving advice or offering solutions. When we prematurely suggest solutions, we quit listening. Giving advice is the normal pattern and a reason we seldom listen well or receive good listening. Just listen and tell the storyteller what you heard. If you are working in a group, empower a member of your group to gently stop any attempt to give advice.

In the first round:

"A" will tell the story.

"B" will listen for and write down what is heard about the facts of the situation.

"C" will listen for and note what is heard about feelings.

"D" will listen for and record what is heard about needs.

"E" will listen for and make notes about the desired outcomes.

After the story is finished, make your way around the circle: "B" will share what was heard about the facts, "C" about feelings, "D" about needs, and "E" about the outcomes desired.

The process works best when people keep their feedback to the storyteller succinct so the process does not bog down. Make the responses clear and to the point. The rotations should move fairly quickly so everyone has a chance to be heard. This is especially a warning for the extroverts who will want to talk a lot or try to tell their own story when they are not in the role of storyteller. Appointing a facilitator to keep the process moving along is recommended.

When the first round is finished, rotate to the next story-teller. Avoid trying to fix anything, however strong the temptation. "B" becomes the storyteller. "C" listens for the facts. "D" listens for feelings. "E" listens for needs. "A" listens for the outcomes desired.

Follow the pattern below for subsequent rounds.

Roles:

0=storyteller
Level 1=facts
Level 2=feelings
Level 3=needs
Level 4=desired outcomes

Rotations:

	A	B	C	D	E	(group members)
Round 1:	0	1	2	3	4	
Round 2:	4	0	1	2	3	
Round 3:	3	4	0	1	2	
Round 4:	2	3	4	0	1	
Round 5:	1	2	3	4	0	

When all members of the group have been heard, each, in turn, can briefly share what new ideas and understanding the listening produced. After everyone has had a chance to share what they learned, others can offer their perspectives.

Process for Partners (40 minutes): After writing about a troubling situation, each person should divide a piece of paper into four parts. Label the squares: Facts, feelings, needs, and desired outcomes. Decide who will be the first storyteller.

As one person is telling the story, the other listens at each of the levels. In the appropriate squares, the listener records what is heard about facts, feelings, needs, and desired outcomes. Short notations are sufficient to jog the memory while giving feedback.

After the story is told, the listener can seek more information before giving feedback. If there are parts of the story that seem sketchy, ask for more information. Seeking more information will allow you to fill in the story and will give the storyteller a clearer idea of the situation when you share what you heard.

When you have satisfactory notes in each area, reveal what you heard, starting with the facts, then going through feelings, needs, and desired outcomes. Do not try to fix the problem.

When that round is finished, the second person gets to be the storyteller and the process is repeated.

When the exercise is completed, each storyteller can share what was learned from the feedback. Then, the partner's perspectives can be offered.

Through practice, we learn to listen at the four levels. By hearing more, more of the person becomes known to us so our understanding expands and deepens. By sharing what we hear, others become more aware of their depth and develop a clearer grasp of their situations. Through deep listening, we develop closer human contact. "I don't really listen," Mandy said. "I just wait for an opportunity to have my say. Today, I realized how important it is to listen in order to understand someone. Without that understanding, there's really no relationship."

Woo Master:
"Woo Master has four ears
to hear depth of person's song,
then person is fully known."

Chapter 17

Speaking To Be
Fully Understood

By learning to listen at the four levels, we prepare ourselves to communicate more deeply so others will more fully understand us. When speaking to someone about an important issue, we start by stating the facts of the situation, then express our feelings about it. Going deeper, our needs are stated, followed by the changes we would like to see. By speaking deeply, we assume responsibility for expressing more completely who we are in the situation.

Imagine speaking at depth when we are communicating love and appreciation to someone. How many times do we say "I love you" or "I appreciate you" without explaining why? Consider taking your mate, mother, father, son, daughter, or another special person to dinner. Over dinner express your love and appreciation, and fully explain why.

Woo Master:
*"Expressing love is like fertilizing plants.
Both make things grow."*

Individual Process (25 minutes): Draw a horizontal line across a page. In the upper part, write the names of people to whom you want to communicate love and appreciation. It might be your mate, a parent, daughter, son, sister, brother, friend, neighbor, someone at work, or at your place of worship. Take a few minutes to complete this work.

Below, identify people you need to speak to about a problem in your relationship.

Using the four levels of communication, write a letter to one of the people to whom you want to express love and appreciation.

Start with a brief description of how you see the facts of your relationship.

Express your feelings about the person.

Identify what she or he does to satisfy your needs.

Note changes you would like to see in the relationship to deepen it.

As you close your letter, ask the person to share how they are feeling about you by asking them: "How do you experience our relationship? What are your feelings about me? Are there any needs of yours I help to satisfy? How would you like our relationship to change so it deepens?"

When your letter is finished, decide if you want to send it or whether you would rather speak directly to the person. Make a decision about when you will do that. (Look at the other names of people toward whom you would like to express love and appreciation. Circle the names of those you intend to contact.)

> *It is up to you to speak deeply*
> *enough to be fully understood.*

If you are working with a partner or group, share your letters, reading them as if the person for whom you feel love and appreciation is present. Discuss how it felt to speak deeply.

Individual Process (25 minutes): Write a letter to one of the people you want to talk to about a problem in your relationship. In the letter, incorporate the following "sandwich technique," so you establish the person's willingness to listen. This simple technique, borrowed from Toastmaster's International, prevents the automatic "defensive" reaction of the listener and, by noticing what is positive and negative in the situation, it captures more of the truth.

Sandwich Technique:

Slice of bread: Say something positive about the person or the relationship. For example, "I really appreciate our relationship and you. I value you a lot. I want to create more understanding between us so our relationship can get even better." Say whatever is true for you.

Meat or veggies: Consider taking responsibility for the problem. Do this by using "I" rather than "you" statements. For example, "I have a problem that I'm trying to solve. Although it arose from something you said, I know it's an issue within me. I'd like you to listen carefully to what I'm going through. After you hear me, I will listen carefully to what you want to say. Is this okay with you?" If the person responds positively, start with a brief description of how you see the facts of the situation, describe your feelings, share your needs, and be clear about what you would like to alter in the relationship to improve it.

Next slice of bread: End on something positive about the person or the relationship. "I love you a lot and see this situation as a way to deepen our relationship. I want to hear your perspective on the issues now, so we can begin thinking about creating some changes together."

Write your letter with the sandwich technique as a guideline and cover the four levels of speaking.

When you have finished, make a choice about whether you will follow up with action. If the choice is "Yes," establish a time for calling the person to set up a meeting.

If you are working with a partner or group, read your letters to each other and describe your intentions to act.

Optional Group Process (50 minutes): You will need five people. Adjust the process if there are fewer or more than five. Form a circle. Relying on the letter, the goal of the speaker is to communicate at the four levels using the sandwich technique. The role of the other members is to listen for and encourage depth of speaking. The important question they will ask: "Would you tell me more about...?"

Roles:

0=speaker

1=facts: Would you tell me more about the situation as you see it?

2=feelings: Would you tell me more about your feelings?

3=needs: Would you tell me more about your needs?

4=outcomes desired: Would you tell me more about the changes in the relationship you would like to see?

Rotations:

	A	B	C	D	E	(Group members)
Round 1:	0	1	2	3	4	
Round 2:	4	0	1	2	3	
Round 3:	3	4	0	1	2	
Round 4:	2	3	4	0	1	
Round 5:	1	2	3	4	0	

When taking the speaker's role, rely on the details of your letter. Speak as if the person were present. The other members of the group will listen from the four levels.

In Round 1, "A" will be speaking, "B" will listen for the facts, "C" for feelings, "D" for needs, and "E" for changes in the relationship the speaker desires. If they feel the speaker has not covered a level fully, they can ask for more information. The listeners will then share what they heard without trying to fix the situation.

When Round 1 is over, go to Round 2, when "B" will be the speaker. Follow the rotations noted above for the remaining rounds.

Select someone in your group to maintain the pace, so

everyone has a chance to speak. Empower that person to put a stop to anyone attempting to offer a solution or to dominate communication within the group. Offering suggestions about peoples' situations can occur after the speaking portion of the process is completed.

While speaking deeply usually produces good results, Jack discovered that the approach did not work with his boss, who responded angrily: "Who are you to tell me how to run this business?" When Jack was asked what he learned from the experience, he replied: "When I have my own business, I will never do that because it's stupid. I would seek advice from my employees because the goal of a manager is to make the organization work. Getting feedback from people who know about the day-to-day operation would be smart."

Recess of the mind: Close your eyes and reflect on how deeply you communicate. What new possibilities emerged from this work?

Woo Master:
"Listen deeply, speak deeply, understand.
Then, soil cultivated for creating changes
and solutions together. I see light. Happy day!"

Many of us have no clear strategy for adding improvements to our relationships or for solving problems and more serious relationship meltdowns. Attempts to change our relationships may be dominated by complaint. Resolving problems may turn into blaming, trying to be right, and struggles for control. An alternative is the strategy of two or more people co-creating ideas to make a change or solve a problem. The point of co-creating changes and solutions is not to dwell on the past, but to work cooperatively with attention clearly on the present and future.

Individual Process (15 minutes): Think of a relationship you would like to improve or one with a problem you would like to resolve. This might be with a mate, child, parent, sister, brother, boss, or co-worker. Decide whether you want your work to focus on adding an improvement or solving a problem.

What strategy do you use to make positive changes in your relationship or solve problems together?

How effective is your method?

How would you change it?

Share what you discovered with your partner or group.

> *Co-creating involves two or more people*
> *with the same tools remodeling a relationship*
> *or fixing a problem. Everyone has a hand*
> *in creating the result.*

Work in the following chapter is a special opportunity to co-create solutions and changes with a person or persons in a relationship with you.

Chapter 18

fixing And Improving Relationships

*7*his chapter includes a special exercise for co-creating ideas with a person or persons in a relationship with you. For example, family members, roommates, or co-workers can be invited to participate, if you want to do group work. The exercise should be done outside the normal course you have been following, working alone or with a partner or group. In preparation for the exercise, decide who you will invite and make arrangements to meet. Be clear about the focus of the work. Is your goal to improve the relationship by adding something positive to it, to solve a problem, or both? In advance of your work together, give a copy of this chapter to the person(s) you have chosen. Also, consider making Chapters 16 and 17 available in order to cultivate an atmosphere of deep listening and speaking.

When we enter the spirit of co-creating ideas, we stop looking into the past to establish blame. Instead, we work in the present to improve the relationship or seek a solution to a problem. Participation is equal. First one person, then the other, contributes, each playing off the other's ideas. Co-creating options in this way makes the outcome into a mutual creation, since each person contributes to it. The following process is set up for two people, but it can be adapted to group work, as noted.

Woo Master:
*"'Goodwill' is like ball in game of baseball.
Without it, nothing positive happens."*

Process for Partners and a Group (indefinite time period): Find a comfortable place to meet, where distractions are limited. Sit beside each other so you are facing in the same direction. Setting up the situation in this way establishes informality, comfort, and cooperation. In a group situation, seek an informal setting where people can comfortably sit together rather than the meeting room with a table.

■ Communicate deeply. Spend time listening and speaking deeply to each other to establish a mutual understanding of the potential of the relationship or your perspectives on a problem that needs fixing. Use the sandwich technique of coaching if necessary. Cover facts, feelings, needs, and desired outcomes. After greater understanding is achieved, agree to co-create changes or solutions together.

■ Identify areas where positive additions to the relationship might improve it or, if you are dealing with a conflict, the problems that need to be addressed. Convey your ideas by taking turns asking questions. If you are looking to remodel the relationship to improve it, you might ask: "How could we increase playfulness between us?" If you are going to solve a problem, the question might be: "How can we solve the problem of getting the household chores done on time?" You may want to jot the questions down. Then, establish an agreement about the key questions before starting and decide which you want to deal with first, second, and third.

If you are going to work on a problem where emotion may surface, decide how you will handle it in advance. If it is anger, will you take a time out from the process? Work your way through it? Give each other permission to express it? Decide not to allow it? Make a decision about what to do about anger at the outset. If you are working in a group, have someone guide the process, so emotional outbursts are handled according to your agreement.

- Generate options to improve the relationship or fix the problem. As you explore the first question, relax and be receptive to the possibility of creating ideas you had not anticipated. Taking turns, generate as many ideas as possible. They can be amusing possibilities to enlighten up the atmosphere. Invite your minds to play so co-creating becomes enjoyable, even fun. Write your ideas down on a large piece of paper.

When working in a group, go around the circle, giving each person a chance to generate an idea or pass. This approach gives everyone an opportunity to contribute and, as the rounds continue, new and sometimes comical ideas may develop. An outrageous idea can sometimes be modified into a constructive option.

- Evaluate your ideas. When you have run out of ideas, examine the options you have written and circle your most promising ones. If you are working in a group, the facilitator insures that everyone participates in identifying the best possibilities.

- Choose options to try. Is there an approach or two that you could agree to try? Which one would you like to pursue first? What will each of you do? How will you do it? When will you do it? If you are working in a group, achieve agreement about your best options and what approach you want to try first.

■ Follow up. Make a commitment to discuss your results. Set a day and time for the meeting. If you discover that an idea has not worked, modify it so it works better, or co-create another one. Keep working together until the changes are made or the problem is solved.

My wife and I learned the value of co-creating when our daughters were teenagers. As most parents of teenagers, we had an intense conflict with them about how late they could stay out at night. At first, we laid down an ultimatum about when they had to be home. They fought against that decision because what was "late" to us was not "late" to them. This problem continued to be a source of conflict in our relationship, until it dawned on my wife and me that our approach was not working.

We invited our daughters to a family meeting. Everyone shared their feelings about the problem and what their needs were in the situation. This deepened our mutual understanding of what "late" meant to them and to us. Options were discussed fully in terms of our feelings and needs. Everyone became more flexible in their positions. My wife and I agreed that our daughters could stay out later than our first ultimatum and they promised to come home earlier than they wanted. We also added an agreement that, when something unexpected made them later, they would call us, whatever the hour. This agreement worked through their teenaged years, partly because we created it together.

To get an agreement that worked, my wife and I had to accept more insecurity. This diminished as we saw repeatedly that our daughters came home safely in the middle of the night. Through this experience, we learned that solving problems together was better than ultimatums in developing a good relationship with our daughters. By inviting them to help resolve the problem, they felt more honor-bound to respect our joint decision. We continued this process of co-creating solutions to problems afterwards. Family meetings for this purpose became regular occurrences in our lives.

Some people think of their relationships as contests. This picture sets the tone for struggles of dominance, makes for bitterness, and can undermine love. Is there another way to think of relationships so love can grow and not just survive? Could our relationships be considered playgrounds? Artful encounters? Co-creating provides a way of transforming our relationships so play and art can live between people. When we succeed in transforming our relationships in this way, we also deepen our capacity to love and be loved.

Woo Master:
"When eyes at same level,
better chance for love to flourish."

Chapter 19

Cleaning Up Relationships

Imagine an oil painting showing people carrying corpses on their backs as they walk down a road. They are weighted down, so there is no possibility they could dance. Sharp bends in their knees convey an impression of the heavy weight they carry. Many of us live this way. We bear the past on our backs like corpses. The past is sometimes so heavy that we can hardly move, so the present is tainted with unhappy memories and the future is neglected. With that burden, we cannot dance and our life may have little joy.

What creates the weight of this burden? Essentially four things: Resentment, guilt, lack of acceptance, and unfinished business. We resent what we think others have done to us and feel guilty for what we did to others. We resist accepting what happened and dwell on relationships that were never completed.

Woo Master:
"I do not walk backwards looking at where I have been, but look ahead to where I am going."

Forgiveness

When we have been unkind or cruel to someone, we store up guilt that becomes part of the weight from the past that we carry. If we feel someone has hurt us, we build up resentment and shoulder that burden. To reduce the weight, we can seek forgiveness from those we have hurt or forgive those who have hurt us. Forgiveness arises from knowing that everyone will occasionally say the wrong thing, lose their tempers, and make bad judgments.

■ Seeking forgiveness

Individual Process (15 minutes): Think about what you still feel guilty about from your past. In your journal, note things you did or failed to do for which you would welcome forgiveness.

List the people from whom you would like forgiveness. Select one person from those noted and describe how you will apologize. If possible, decide when and by what means you will seek forgiveness. If communicating with that person is impossible, imagine asking for and receiving forgiveness.

■ Forgiving others

Individual Process (15 minutes): On another page, list the names of people who hurt you that you are willing to consider forgiving. In deciding who to add, think about who you are still feeling resentment towards.

Looking through your list, select one person to forgive. Note what it would take to grant forgiveness. For example, perhaps "generosity" comes to mind.

Develop a brief statement of forgiveness to that person.

Decide when and how you will express it.

■ Forgiving yourself

Individual Process (15 minutes): Note things you did or failed to do that you are still feeling guilty about.

Select an item from your list and briefly describe what it would take for you to forgive yourself. For example, it might be to abandon the idea that "The guilt I feel is my deserved punishment."

Have the experience of forgiving yourself.

If you are working with a partner or group, share your experiences of forgiveness.

We have successfully forgiven others when we no longer resent them for what they did to us. We have successfully forgiven ourselves when we no longer persecute ourselves for what we did.

A man was sorting out his life as he was preparing to die. When his sister visited him, he handed her a gift. She was surprised when she opened the box and discovered a chocolate rabbit with long ears. Completely baffled, she asked her brother to explain. "Do you remember the year when someone ate the ears off your chocolate Easter bunny and you never discovered the culprit? Well, I was the culprit and I've been feeling guilty about that ever since. This gift is my way of saying I'm sorry, so I can quit feeling guilty about it. Will you forgive me?"

147

Woo Master:
"Children forgive and forget.
Grown ups forget to forgive."

Acceptance

Some of us constantly reconstruct the past, thinking of all the ways it might have been different, then complaining about it. In contrast, by realizing that the past cannot be changed, we can accept what happened, even if we cannot forgive others or ourselves. Accepting the painful event as a part of our story, the weight of the burden we carry is reduced, so we feel freer to live in the moment.

Acceptance arises from the mind's ability
to quit resisting what it cannot change.
Since the past cannot be changed,
there is nothing back there that cannot be accepted.

Individual Process (15 minutes): Become aware of something someone did to you that you cannot forgive but can now accept as part of your story. Write out your acceptance.

Recall an experience when you mistreated someone and, while you cannot forgive yourself, you can accept it as a mistake you made and learned from. Write out your acceptance.

If you are working with a partner or group, share what you experienced about acceptance.

Woo Master:
"Many obstacles disappear when embraced."

Completion

There is usually unfinished business in our past. It might include completing a communication with someone from a past conflict or conveying love or appreciation to someone that was never expressed.

Individual Process (25 minutes): Write a letter completing a communication with someone in your life about a conflict or your unexpressed feelings of love or appreciation.

If you are working with a partner or group, share with each other.

Jennifer chose to write a letter to her grandmother. Her grandmother had died suddenly, so there had been no opportunity for Jennifer to express her love and appreciation for the person she called her guide, comfort, and inspiration. In her letter, which she had the courage to read aloud, she poured out her heart, stopping at intervals to gain her composure. By the end, many who listened were in tears. With relief but also a hint of embarrassment, Jennifer ended with words that sounded almost like a quiet prayer, "Perhaps I can go on now."

We know that we have reduced the weight of the past when our thinking shifts from a preoccupation with past events to the present and future. The most tangible effects of this change are less resentment and guilt, a reduction of suffering, and a greater sense of well-being.

A new idea for an oil painting emerges, quite different from the one depicting people carrying corpses on their backs. Now, the canvas shows people dancing away from the corpses they have dropped. On the clothing of the dancing people you can see the words "Forgiveness," "Acceptance," and "Completion." Some are smiling; others sing. Free from the past, this is the beginning of the celebration.

Woo Master:
"Add bubbles to thinking.
Lighter mind creates lighter life."

Part IV

Developing Balance, Wholeness, And Wisdom

A student had come under the guidance of a spiritual teacher who he had heard was extraordinary. Day after day he watched the teacher, but the teacher did not seem extraordinary at all. In fact, he appeared to be an average person. Finally, he said to the teacher: "I've heard so many stories about what an extraordinary teacher you are, but I see you behaving each day as an ordinary person. What am I to think?" The teacher smiled, "Yes, I'm very ordinary. All I do is watch my students as if they were walking down a road. I just say, 'Too far to the right, too far to the left'. Very simple." Very simple perhaps, but to know when his students were out of balance, the teacher had to be in balance himself. Ordinary or extraordinary?

Woo Master:
"Becoming balanced is key to happy and
harmonious life. Hard to push over balanced
person who has both feet on ground,
like trying to push over tree with deep roots."

Woo is the state of equilibrium where the opposites within us have been so fully embraced, the conflict between them is transcended. This puts us on both feet, so we are able to move to the right or left with equal ease. It is this balance and flexibility that puts the little smile on the Woo Master's face. How we find that balance and create that little smile is the work we do next. As the basis of that work, we draw on Carl Jung's thinking about individuation, the process of becoming a whole person.

In *Modern Man in Search of a Soul*, Jung argued that a great deal of human suffering in our age arises from the loss of a meaningful connection to the soul. He equates the soul with the Self, the archetype of wholeness that exists within all of us. The most powerful symbol of the Self is the mandala, an exquisite artistic image of wholeness and psychological integration. "Persona" and "shadow" are ideas that form the basis of Jung's thinking about becoming individuated.

"Persona" is the self-image we present socially. Our social mask, it combines the personal attributes we emphasize so we are seen in a positive light by others. Our group's values will influence what we accentuate, but, unless we have chosen an anti-social lifestyle, our persona will include the positive side of the opposites. Since we want to be accepted to feel good, we create self-images that earn praise from those whose opinions we most value. What is withheld and often repressed makes its way into the personal unconscious to become a part of our "shadow," which includes the neglected and despised parts of ourselves.

The goal of shadow work is to become aware of what we have pushed underground, so the opposites within us can be brought into sharper focus. Through this effort, we learn to embrace our opposing tendencies and live between them in

152

their natural tension. This shift to the center must inevitably change our self-image, because we have to expand our sense of self to encompass our dual nature. This is what Jung meant by "enlargement of personality." This expansion of personality makes living in balance possible. It allows us to experience the rhythm of our wholeness. Then we are able to live with a simple kind of wisdom.

Chapter 20

Life Out Of Balance

*T*here is a scene in the early Star Wars trilogy where Yoda, the Jedi Master, takes Luke Skywalker to the edge of a primordial forest for training. Luke is afraid: "What will I find in there?" Yoda, with a knowing glimmer in his eye, responds: "You will find yourself." Star Wars is about individuation, confronting the shadow and transforming the darkness into light. We may not like what we find in the darkness, but recognizing what is there is a crucial step in discovering the possibility of living between the opposites within our minds. From that knowledge, wholeness of being emerges, so living in balance is easier.

Woo Master:
"When monsters under bed are called out to play, what scared us runs quickly away."

Individual Process (5 minutes): Stand on one leg. Remain that way for a few moments. Hop around on it. Do that until you tire.

What did you notice while standing on one foot? Was maintaining balance difficult, even painful? Did you tire easily?

Now stand on both feet and move your weight gently from one foot to another. Be aware of how this experience is different from trying to balance on one foot.

What did you experience? Was it easier to balance? Did you feel a rhythm develop as you moved your weight from one foot to another?

By dancing between the opposites in yourself, you learn to avoid the extremes of your nature, so your life remains in balance.

> *By looking carefully, we discover a*
> *strength in every weakness and a*
> *weakness in every strength.*

Individual Process (30 minutes): Make two columns on a journal page. In the left column, note the ways you want to be perceived by others. For example, perhaps "confident" and "attractive" may come to mind.

Next, alongside the attributes in column one, use column two for recording their opposites. For instance, "lack confidence" would be the opposite of "confident." The qualities in column two are aspects of your personal shadow.

Taking each shadow aspect in turn, briefly describe in your journal how you possess it and what contribution it makes to your life. For example, a person might describe how "lack of confidence" prevents arrogance.

Next, read your opposing tendencies aloud. As you do, feel your sense of self expand to encompass your dual nature and wholeness.

Movement option: After writing out your opposites, stand on both feet. Let us assume that one pair is "I'm informed" and "I'm ignorant." Shift your weight to one foot while saying "I'm informed," then shift your weight to the other foot as you say "I'm ignorant." Use this movement for each pair of opposites.

Notice the balance and gentle rhythm that arise as you shift your weight back and forth. Expand your sense of self to experience the rhythm of your wholeness.

Recess of the mind: After you have integrated the opposites, consider how balancing on both feet might change your way of living and being. What new sense of self emerges? What new freedom is possible? Close your eyes and quietly reflect on these questions.

If you are working with a partner or group, share your discoveries. Discuss how you will integrate this knowledge into your life.

Woo Master:
"Perfection lives on one foot:
wholeness on two."

Optional Process for Partners or a Group (30 minutes): Create pairs. Follow the preliminary steps above. When the shadow attributes are fully recorded, take turns explaining to each other how you possess a particular shadow attribute and what contribution it makes to your life. Give examples.

Go back and forth until all shadow characteristics have been covered. If you want to omit one or two, ask yourself why. (This is a difficult process. It may embarrass you because you are having to reveal things about yourself you have learned are "bad." Know that you have the choice not to share everything if it is too difficult.)

At the end, discuss what the process revealed and what you learned from it.

In shadow work, we shift from the person's emphasis on always looking good, with its perfectionist overtones, to the goal of individuation, which is integrating the opposites. Instead of trying so hard to appear confident and to hide our lack of confidence, we embrace our dual tendencies and live on two feet. "I'm a person who can be confident or lack confidence, depending on the situation. Both are parts of me." Admitting the two sides, we achieve greater wholeness.

Woo Master:
"Life is sloppy. Wear rubber boots."

Life is sloppy. We long for order in our thinking, the categorical "Yes" or "No" without doubt, but conflict is closer to the daily reality of our inner life. When we examine our thoughts and feelings honestly, we often discover opposing tendencies. We may find ourselves automatically resisting the confusion and doubt that arise from this realization. In contrast, living between the opposites while wearing rubber boots, we embrace the confusion and doubt as part of our wholeness. Instead of living in a one-sided way, we play with the idea that we are of two minds.

Making Room For Contradiction

As we begin living between the opposites, it becomes clear that we are of two minds about many things. Opposing tendencies exist within us naturally, yet our culture encourages us to avoid contradictions. To be caught in a contradiction means that we lose face and the argument.

Suffering arises because we think that having contradictory thoughts is a sign of confusion and weakness. When we realize that our nature is to be of two minds, contradictions can be expressed freely. You will have an opportunity to experience a type of freedom most people avoid. You get to be contradictory!

Individual Process (15 minutes): On a journal page, note the contradictions that exist within you. Some may exist around social issues. Others may be contradictory inner drives. For example, "I love control, but there is a part of me that hates the responsibility of it." Feel the freedom of being a person of contradiction.

If you are working with a partner or group, share your contradictions.

Jung pointed out that shadow work requires a firm ethical stance to prevent the occurrence of antisocial and destructive behavior. The goal of shadow work is to understand our dual nature in order to create balance and wholeness, not to unleash our aggressive instincts on to the world. A great shortcoming of human beings is that we are largely ignorant of our shadows. Unaware of our unconscious, it dominates us from the interior and can lead us onto destructive paths. For example, by automatically projecting our shadows onto others, we can rationalize hating and wanting to kill them. As an ethical stand, shadow work puts a stop a stop to mindless aggression.

Beyond these larger issues, there is another important reason to embrace the opposites and to develop more balance between them. It is our own well-being, because we suffer from living in a one-sided way. As we expand our identity to embrace the opposites, we allow more of ourselves to live and take less seriously the issues that troubled us before. We discover our "right size," which is not too big and not too little. "Just right," Goldilocks would say.

By realizing that "ordinary" is your real size, you develop greater access to freedom and the chance to develop a more balanced and healthy sense of individuality. No longer having to prove your greatness to compensate for your feelings of inadequacy, you can relax and live more at ease. With nothing to prove, get, defend, and hide, you develop a gentle kind of inner power, Woo power. When someone says to you, "My, that was a stupid thing to say," you respond, "Yes, I can be stupid." Whatever people say about you, you can find a grain of truth in it. Living in greater wholeness of being, others can no longer reach into your heart and crush it because, like your inner Woo Master, you have the wisdom to understand that being ordinary is good enough. That acceptance is what puts the little smile on the Woo Master's face.

Woo Master:
*"Knowing our real size, who can touch us
with harsh words? We say, 'Yes, I am that'.
Then we smile and bow to our dual nature."*

Chapter 21

Shadow Projection

*P*eople sometimes project what they despise about themselves onto others, and then dislike or hate them for it. At
other times, they may project positive qualities, especially
onto leaders and cultural heroes, and then idolize them for
it. In the daily news, we see evidence of projection operating worldwide. It produces great suffering when it spawns
hate and violence, and becomes a source of community
when followers create a divine leader to adore and serve. In
less extreme forms, projection of the shadow operates in our
daily lives. How many people must carry our projected
shadow so we can remain unconscious of our negative and
positive qualities?

When I was in high school, I disliked Rob intensely. I created stories in my mind about how he was self-centered,
egotistical, and aggressive. Occasionally, I would bring
Rob up in conversations with my friends and make dis-
paraging remarks about him. During that time, I needed a
job and was hired at a local super market. Arriving at work
on my first day, I was surprised to discover Rob in the back
room putting on an apron. I learned that we would be working together. I considered quitting, but I needed the job.

Over the next few weeks, my animosity toward Rob disappeared as I got to know him. I discovered that he was not

self-centered, but was sensitive to other peoples' needs. He was not egotistical, but was caring and playful. He was not aggressive, but cooperative in every way. All the beliefs I had developed about him were false. Before long, we were the very best of friends. We spent many wonderful times together over the next several years.

Who was Rob? Not what my uninformed mind told me he was. I had projected my self-centeredness, my egotism, and my aggressiveness onto him. Then, I disliked him for what I could not stand about myself. Only much later in my life was I able to consciously integrate the negative shadow parts that Rob had unwittingly carried for me. They are part of my dual nature.

Woo Master:
"If I can make monster out of you,
I do not have to see monster in me."

Individual Process (25 minutes): Divide a journal page in half. On one half, note things that annoy you about others. Those would be attributes that might cause you to avoid or dislike them. Circle four qualities that make you particularly irritated.

On the second half, note the positive qualities of people that cause you to admire them. Afterwards, circle the four most important qualities.

In your journal, write about how you possess each of the four traits that irritate you in others. Describe how they appear and how you feel when they emerge against your wishes.

How could you accept those negative aspects of yourself?

How would acceptance create a better balance between the opposites within you?

How would greater balance affect who you declare yourself to be?

When that work is completed, write about how you possess each of the four qualities you admire in others. Explain when those qualities appear in you and how you feel about yourself when they do.

How could you more fully accept those positive qualities?

How would that create a better balance between the opposites within you?

How would greater balance influence how you view yourself?

Write a poem or do some free writing to express the new sense of self that emerges from taking back your projections.

If you are working with a partner or group, share your insights and writing.

We are already whole, but our one-sidedness keeps us from seeing it.

Susan detested lazy people. When she thought about taking back her projection, she admitted that she hated the lazy part of herself. She was a perfectionist. She worked hard accomplishing the tasks on her daily lists. She could not allow herself to be lazy. "When I saw why I despise lazy people, I realized that what I hate I desperately need. I need to take a break from my crazy schedule and to be lazy at times. Then, maybe I won't be so stressed out."

At times, we may also resist accepting the positive qualities we project onto others. "One of the things I give away is wisdom," Randy admitted. "I have a hard time thinking of myself as wise. By believing I don't have wisdom, I don't try to be wise. So, I'm taking my wisdom back. 'Sage Randy'. I like that."

Woo Master:
"Better chance of thinking like sage when you call yourself one."

Chapter 22

Cultivating Wisdom

*W*isdom is not a word we hear or use very often. In fact, it is one of three neglected questions. Often, when facing a problem, "What is the right thing to do here?" comes immediately to mind. This question engages our values or interests. Often, we do not think to ask:

"What is the creative thing to do here?"
"What is the kind thing to do?"
"What is the wise course?"

As soon as a neglected question is raised, the mind begins seeking appropriate answers. "What is the wise thing to do here?" invites the mind to search for wise options. By posing this simple question, wisdom is nurtured in our daily lives. By consciously cultivating it, we eventually become wiser. Through this gardening effort, our lives come to reflect more fully the wisdom of our inner Woo Master.

Woo Master:
"Wisdom is like plant.
Cultivate it, then watch it grow."

Individual Process (10 minutes): On a journal page, let your mind play with the question: "What are the attributes of wisdom?" Jot down your ideas quickly.

Circle what you regard as the most significant attributes.

Using them, write a short poem or paragraph that captures your thinking about wisdom.

Note the names of people who seem to have the kind of wisdom you identified.

If you are working with a partner or group, share your views of wisdom and your examples of wise people.

Consulting Your Inner Wise Person

To ensure that the question about wisdom is asked, make it a common practice to consult your inner wise person when facing a problem.

Uno has been my wise person for many years. He is a gardener who lives in a small, modest cabin surrounded by lush gardens of fruit, vegetables, and flowers. He is very wise and lives to make things grow. When I have a problem I am struggling with, I go to him. Some days, he teaches while he is pruning or planting. At other times, he invites me into his cabin for tea. He speaks simply, although sometimes his teaching is so subtle I have to contemplate it for days afterwards. On occasion, he does not speak at all, but reveals a lesson by doing something.

Once, when I asked for wise counsel about a problem, he took me into the garden, dug a deep hole, pointed to the bottom, then smiled. After thinking about what he had done, I realized that the wise course was to dig more deeply into my problem until I understood it at all levels. Then I would know how to handle it. I did that and it worked.

Uno is not a real person, but a creation of my imagination. I brought him into my life at a time when I needed more wisdom. Now, you will have an opportunity to create your wise person, so you can bring more wisdom into your life.

Individual Process (30 minutes): Creating your wise person is an act of imagination. Write a brief description of a person you would like to consult regularly.

When your wise person is described in enough detail, decide on a problem. What questions will you ask about it? Note those.

In a moment, you will close your eyes and consult your wise person. This will be a act of imagination, so let your creativity shape it.

When you close your eyes, create a scene where you would like your wise person to live. When that place is created in your imagination, make contact with your wise person. When you are together, introduce your problem and ask your first question. The answer may be obvious or you may have to actively discover the meaning of what is said or done.

Pursue your other questions.

Ask your wise person whether he or she has questions to ask you.

At the end, express your appreciation.

Now, close your eyes and begin.

When you are finished, write about the wisdom you received and how it affected your orientation to the problem.

If you are working with a partner or group, share what you learned.

After consulting with his wise person, Evan approached me. "Someday I'm going to call you and I'll be in some kind of distress," he said. "When I call, I want you to tell me: 'Remember that you're carrying wisdom in your pocket'. Tell me to take it out, say 'Goodbye', then hang up."

Finding our wise person validates the existence of our own wisdom. It is in our pockets. It was always there, but we failed to ask the right question to retrieve it. Now we will practice reaching in and taking our wisdom out.

How will you use the wisdom in your pocket?

How will you develop a closer relationship with your wise person?

Woo Master:
"Warmth makes flowers bloom.
Wisdom makes life bloom."

Chapter 23

7houghts Can, 7orture You

Woo Master:
"Mind is best movie in town.
Sometimes beautiful story.
Sometimes horror flick."

Some of us have a torture chamber within our minds that we visit frequently. The structure of the torture chamber rests on the belief that our negative thoughts are true. For example, "I'm not a likeable person" is just a thought. Yet, if we believe it is true, we give it substance and then torture ourselves with it.

You have undoubtedly watched a movie where you became so engrossed in the plot that you forgot you were watching fiction. You were so fully drawn into the experience that you lost your capacity as an observer. Without that detachment, you probably became emotionally absorbed in the drama.

Many of us relate to our thoughts this way. Thinking they are true, we become swept up in the emotions they create.

Affected by the emotions, we lose the capacity for detachment. When we realize that our thoughts may not be true, we are able to get in the "director's chair" and make choices rather than being in automatic emotional reactions. The director's chair symbolizes the part of us that can observe thoughts with neutrality, so we can control them rather than being under their control.

Woo Master:
"Sheep do not herd sheep dog,
but other way around.
Thoughts do not herd Woo Master,
but other way around."

Individual Process (5 minutes): Sit with your eyes closed and watch your thoughts. Notice how they come and go. Instead of thinking your thoughts are true, experience them as just thoughts.

When we realize that thoughts are just thoughts, it is easier to get into the director's chair. When we do, we create an opportunity to manage any thought that torments us. When a thought makes us suffer, we can intervene by making one of the following decisions.

Reject it.
Reverse it.
Replace it with a positive thought.

If the thought emerges, "I'm not interesting," we can simply reject it. We can reverse it: "I am interesting." We can replace it with a positive thought: "I'm going to become more interesting by sharing more of myself." Through these choices, we give up being the victims of torturing thoughts and become the creators of our mental life.

Individual Process (20 minutes): Being aware of negative thoughts as just thoughts gives us the capacity to manage them. The following is practice.

Write down a thought that makes you suffer.

Reject it. What would emerge in your life if, every time you had this thought, you would give it up? As you write about this question, feel yourself sitting in the director's chair.

Record another thought that makes you suffer.

Reverse it. How does that new thought affect you?

Describe a third thought that makes you suffer.

Replace it with a positive thought. What changes are possible?

If you are working with a partner or group, share the work you did.

Learning how to give up thoughts, reverse them, or create new thoughts is the key step to directing our inner movies. When we learn to direct our thoughts, we edit our inner movies to produce a better life.

Woo Master:
"To increase happiness, remove negative thoughts.
This is recommended diet for tortured mind."

"If, Then"

There are thoughts about the past, present, and future that can also torment us. They are part of the thinking trap "If, then." This little thought, if repeated often enough, can create a conditional life. It is a life that cannot be fully lived because we think we are missing something that is essential for achieving happiness, success, or contentment.

Our lives can be put on hold by conditional thoughts.

About the past: "If I'd come from a happy family, then I'd be happy."

About the present: "If I wasn't so old, then I could start taking cello lessons."

About the future: "If I could retire, I'd be at peace with myself."

Each of these thoughts stops us from having the life we want now. We may quit seeking happiness, never try the cello, and postpone the experience of inner peace. All because of "If, then" thoughts that we believe are true.

Individual Process (20 minutes): Divide a journal page into three parts. Label them "Past," "Present," "Future."

In each part, record "If, then" thoughts you have.

Circle the thoughts that have the greatest power to hold you back from pursuing the life you want now.

Take each thought and make one of the following choices:

Reject it.
Reverse it.
Replace it with a positive thought.

Contemplate your work, then make new choices. What will change?

If you are working with a partner or group, share your discoveries.

What if, instead of thinking that our happiness, success, and inner peace had to be postponed, we realized that they are available to us now?

Woo Master:
"Only this moment.
Happiness, success,
peace already present.
Just notice."

Individual Process (10 minutes): We can create emotional states by choosing to enter them.

With eyes closed, experience each of the following states for a few minutes.

Happiness.

Success.

Inner peace.

If you are working with a partner or group, reveal what you

experienced.

When the sheep dog decides to take charge, the sheep respond. When you decide to manage your thoughts, they become more manageable. Imagine a life where you are in charge of your thoughts, rather than the other way around.

Woo Master:
"Change thoughts, change self."

Chapter 24

✒️ears ᴀre ᴏften ᴇxaggerations

here are real dangers. When we experience them, fear is a warning to protect ourselves. But, there are also many fears that are exaggerations of failure or harm. Those are the fears we will address because we have a chance to manage them. When we examine our fears closely, we discover that most of them magnify the probability of bad things happening to us or our loved ones. Some fears, such as the fear of heights, we may never overcome and simply have to accept as part of us. Yet, there are many fears that lose some of their power the moment we realize that they are exaggerations. When we have a fearful thought, we can ask, "How much is my mind just trying to scare me with unrealistic predictions of failure or harm?"

Woo Master:
"Mind loves to scare me.
Paints terrible pictures that stop me in tracks.
I see pictures as fiction, then scare mind right back."

Individual Process (5 minutes): If you were to go back to the beginning of your life and watch it as a movie, how often would you say your fears were realized? About what percentage of the time did your fears come true? Close your eyes, address these questions, and come up with a percentage.

If you are working with a partner or group, share your discoveries.

Most people find that the vast majority of their fears were never actualized. This discovery opens the way for learning how to use the "1% rule" when fear is present.

How the 1% rule works:

When we are experiencing a fear, first we ask whether it is a thought that is magnifying the probability of failure or misfortune.

If we think it is, we ask: "What's the realistic probability that my fear will come true?" Then, we assert that it is 1% or less. (Often, it is close to zero.)

By using the 1% rule as a method of interacting with our fears, we are able to shrink many of them down to fit in the palm of our hand. When they are that small, we can get into the director's chair and choose to reject, reverse, or replace them.

Individual Process (30 minutes): On a page in your journal, record as many of your fears as you can in ten minutes' time. These may be fears related to physical safety, rejection, failure, success, or public speaking, among others.

Next, evaluate your fears:

Put a 1 by any fear that needs more attention for security's sake. Are there real dangers you are not acknowledging and dealing with? To achieve better balance, some of us need to pay closer attention to neglected dangers, so we can protect ourselves more effectively. Examining each of your fears, describe what specific precautions you will take.

Put a 2 by fears that are so irrational and overwhelming it is unlikely that you will be able to change them, but you could embrace them as a part of you. For example, fear of heights. Describe what it will take to accept those fears. How does accepting them make you feel?

Put a 3 by fears that are exaggerations you can manage.

Taking one of your magnified fears, establish the 1% rule.

Next, get into the director's chair and choose to reject it, reverse it, or replace it with a positive thought. What new possibilities emerge?

Repeat this process for your remaining exaggerated fears.

If you are working with a partner or group, share your insights and results.

Rebecca asked: "How can I get my mother, who's a professional worrier, to quit worrying? I tell her she shouldn't worry, but that does no good. So, she suffers." Telling people to stop worrying will not help, unless we teach them about the nature of fear as exaggeration. People who are unable to manage their fearful thoughts will be managed by them. The consequence is suffering and a diminished life. They live in such worry that they miss some of life's joy.

Woo Master:
"When worry is present, no room for smile."

Fears Hold Us Back From Living

Angela was afraid of flying so she held back from pursuing one of her dreams, which was to go to Europe with friends. After a week of using the 1% rule to manage other fears, she ordered her ticket. She went and had a wonderful time. Angela's experience demonstrates how exaggerated fears can keep us from pursuing dreams and opportunities.

When we worry too much, we fall out of balance and our lives lose some of their potential abundance. When we realize how many of our fears never materialize, we worry less, so we are more able to pursue challenges and opportunities. When a fear is sitting in the palm of our hands, it takes less courage to seek the lives we want.

Individual Process (15 minutes): List all the challenges you passed up or the opportunities you let slip by because of unrealistic fears.

Note challenges and opportunities your fears are holding you back from pursuing now. Take each fear and establish the 1% rule, then reject the fear, reverse it, or replace it. What are you now willing to try or pursue more fully?

If you are working with a partner or group, discuss your experiences and any new challenges or opportunities you are ready to pursue.

While fears are an unavoidable part of being human, they can be managed because they are thoughts. Some fears require action when the danger is clear; others will be exaggerations we can keep in check by applying the 1% rule. Learning to manage our fears is important, because we pay a price for excessive worrying, not only in well-being, but in our appreciation of life. For example, Rebecca's mother, an extreme worrier, exaggerates danger in her life. She also contaminates the lives of those she loves with her excessive concerns for safety. She wants them to share her view of life's many dangers, so they will take the precautions she considers necessary for their survival. She believes that she is doing them a favor by constantly warning them to be careful, but think of the consequences in terms of their quality of life.

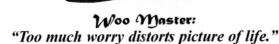

Woo Master:
"Too much worry distorts picture of life."

Fears Diminish By Seeking Evidence

One reason our fears diminish and sometimes disappear is that we test our estimates of disaster against reality and they often prove to be wrong. This is why acting in the face of fear is important. Courage helps us accumulate contradictory evidence to diminish or eliminate our fears. For example, people who fear air travel might need to risk it, so they experience returning home unharmed.

One Spring, I flew to California to visit my family. I sat next to two brothers, who were about nine years old. I could see that the boy next to me was very nervous, so I asked him how he was feeling. He told me he was "really scared" because he had never flown before. He and his brother were going to visit their grandparents alone for the first time.

When the plane was ready to take off, the boy's fear became so great that he began shaking. To comfort him, I took his hand. He smiled in appreciation. He held my hand all the way to California. When the plane shook from turbulence, he squeezed it tightly. I reassured him, telling him that the plane was bouncing on rough air like a car bounces on a rough road. I asked him questions about his life to distract him, but, believing there was a high probability of a plane crash, fear maintained a tight grip on him.

As the plane landed, I watched a look of relief spread over his face. He let go of my hand, smiled, and said: "Now that I know the plane landed, I won't be as afraid when I fly home." By taking the risk of flying, he developed information to contradict his fear. I am sure he has flown many times since and I assume his fear is now more manageable.

Woo Master:
"Life is not as scary as we imagine
or as safe as we want.
That is why it is called 'adventure'."

Chapter 25

No Resistance

Woo Master:
*"Mind is funny thing.
It wants things its way,
but life just laughs
and does what it wants."*

*T*he pizza I had prepared for dinner was done. As I pulled it out of the oven, it slipped off the tin and fell into a heap on the burning hot metal below. I stood there looking at it, saying to myself "Pizza all over oven." After a few seconds of looking at the wreckage, I thought, "Well, I guess it's time to clean it up." As I began scraping it together, removing what was still edible, a question came to me. "What opportunity appears because of this situation? We haven't cleaned the bottom of the oven in a long time." I cleaned the oven and my wife and I ate what was left of the pizza.

When I describe this experience to others, I ask them what they would have done under the circumstances. Many say they would have exploded in anger. One young man said the pizza would have ended up on the wall.

The pizza story reveals another source of suffering that emerges from our normal way of thinking. The cause of this suffering is so subtle we are usually unaware of its influence. We resist the way life appears, which makes us frustrated, irritable, and angry. Our mental templates create this resistance. Our templates are patterns of expectation and desire we use to evaluate our experiences. When a situation conforms to them, we feel satisfied or happy. When it fails, we react automatically by falling into negative feelings and moods.

Do you remember the last time you started a project at home and, instead of it taking the expected 30 minutes, it took four hours? We have many expectations about how much time things should take, then become annoyed because they take much longer. We keep thinking life is suppose to conform to our desires, but, as the Woo Master says, it simply laughs and does what it wants.

Woo Master:
*"Things take as long as they take.
Not one second less or one second more."*

If a situation cannot be changed, irritation, stress, and anger deepen our misery. Just as the pizza all over the oven will not respond to our tirades, neither will life. It does not care what we want; it simply appears the way it does. Instead of resisting circumstances and suffering, we can move into the director's chair. If we cannot change the situation, we give up opposition to it, so our mental suffering stops. When we learn to give up resistance to what we cannot change, life becomes easier and we become more effective.

Individual Process (30 minutes): In your journal, record what you resist but cannot change. Do you resist traffic jams, going to work, or getting older?

Next to each situation you resist, write a word that expresses your emotional response to the situation.

Examining each example, briefly describe how you could change your thinking to stop the resistance.

Without the resistance, do any opportunities appear? For example, when we quit resisting traffic lines at a stop light, the opportunity to relax appears.

Recess of the mind: Take a few minutes to contemplate your insights.

If you are working with a partner or group, share your experiences.

Woo Master:
"'Impatience' is trying to go faster than speed of life."

"So It Is"

"So it is" is a statement we can repeat any time life laughs at us and does what it wants. This simple acknowledgment helps us accept the way life is appearing, then we just deal with it. When we bow down to reality, we create the flexibility to live into our circumstances. Why should we add suffering to what we cannot change? For example, we do not have to make aging more difficult by struggling against the inevitable. Looking at our wrinkles, we can acknowledge their presence, then hear our inner Woo Master say "So it is." In that moment, wisdom emerges to stop turbulence from forming in quiet water.

"So it is" embraces pizza all over the oven, traffic lines, cold days when we are longing for summer, sore joints, and dozens of other things we cannot change, but resist daily. It is simple wisdom, yet its capacity to reduce our suffering is profound. When we quit resisting what we cannot change and just deal with life, we move into positive action so that things get done more easily.

Winnie the Pooh Master:
"No more honey in my jar.
Better go get some."

A group of women who lived together were excited to share an experience with the class. Carol spoke for the group. "Yesterday, we made pizza for dinner. We were thinking about the pizza story, so we carefully took the pizza from the oven. We got it out and were about to put it on the counter when it slipped and fell face down on the floor. We looked at each other in shock. Then, we yelled 'Pizza on floor.' We laughed so hard tears were streaming down our faces. Then, Jackie cried out, 'I see an opportunity to clean floor'. This sent everyone into laughing fits again." Hearing this response to pizza on floor, the Woo Master would smile and say quietly, "Ah, living with greater ease."

Chapter 26

Reducing The Size Of Your Problems

*W*hen we choose lives of high drama, every problem becomes enormous. We transform "molehills" into "mountains," and then we have to scale them. Our thinking produces this life of living crisis and misery. It is a part of the mental torture chamber we construct. Since the mind loves puzzles and challenges, a part of it may even enjoy the soap opera life with its problems, worries, and emotional pain. Yet, there is the choice to make suffering a call to practice. "How is my thinking creating this suffering? What choice would reduce it?" Getting into the director's chair gives us an opportunity to reduce the size of our problems, so we suffer less and become more effective.

Woo Master:
"Easier to carry small packages than big ones."

Individual Process (30 minutes): In your journal, describe a personal issue in your life that seems rather large at the moment.

On the page, draw a small stick figure that represents you. Behind that figure, draw a building the size of the problem you just identified. This will give you an idea of how big the problem seems to you. The building can be a simple rectangle or square.

One way to manage the size of a problem is to see it from the vantage point of a mouse and buffalo. This method is revealed in *Seven Arrows* by Hyemeyohsts Storm. By seeing the problem close up like a mouse or with the far-ranging perspective of the buffalo, we bring all problems into perspective. This increases our ability to deal with them effectively.

For a few minutes, look into the problem from the mouse's point of view. Examine its many facets and nature. Look inside of it. From that close up perspective, note insights that emerge about the problem and how you might approach it.

By seeing with the eyes of the mouse, did your problem become smaller or larger? Increase or decrease the size of your building to reflect what happened.

When the mouse's perspective fails to reduce the size of a problem or makes it larger, seeing from the vantage point of the buffalo may help. Its sweeping view of the plains gives it a broader, longer term perspective on any issue. It is able to see the big picture.

Taking the perspective of the buffalo, examine your problem then write about what you have seen. How does its vantage point shape your thinking and options?

Seeing from the perspective of the buffalo, did your problem become smaller or larger? Change your building's dimensions to correspond to the size of your problem after exploring it from that point of view.

If you are working with a partner or group, share what you learned and how you will use it.

When I catch myself thinking that I have a problem, I ask myself whether it will be engraved on my tombstone. This allows me to step back and see the issue from the buffalo's perspective. I imagine my tombstone, fail to see the problem there, and then say, "This problem is pretty insignificant." Seeing the smaller size of the problem, my concern about it diminishes while my effectiveness to deal with it increases. I have used the image of my tombstone for years as a way of understanding the real size of my problems. Few of them make it onto the tombstone.

Woo Master:
"To change size of problem,
change size of thought behind it."

Chapter 27

Creating Your Life

𝒜wareness, choice, and change are always available to us. When we realize that we have the power to change ourselves, our circumstances, and our lives, we claim the ability to create a new way to live. Instead of living as others do, we can seek a new direction. The Woo Master says: "When old way is not working, new way opens." To equip us for this change, what do we need to create? An empowered identity, a direction for our lives, and ethical principles to guide our behavior along the way. With those in hand, we increase our chances of creating the lives we want.

You have always been special.
There will never be another person like you, ever.

Creating An Empowered Identity

One day, Paul came by to talk. He had a deeply concerned look in his eyes. "What's bothering you?" I asked. "I'm confused because I don't know who I am. I've been searching for my identity for years, but haven't found it. After all my searching, I still don't know who I am and I suffer from not knowing." He was struggling to hold back tears, when I asked "What would your wise person have to say about this?" He closed his eyes.

He sat that way for a couple of minutes, contemplating the question. When he finally opened his eyes, a smile spread across his face. "My wise person put his hand gently on top of my head and looking directing into my eyes, he whispered, 'Don't worry, I don't know who I am either'. Then we laughed together."

In this brief encounter with his own wisdom, Paul tasted freedom. He learned that it is wise not to worry about identity, because there is a playfulness in not knowing who we are and creating who we want to be.

Woo Master:
"When too serious, let smile appear.
In balance, darkness flees.
Then, feet do little dance."

Like Paul, some of us go through life looking for an identity, fail to find it, and suffer. A minor awakening occurs when we realize that there never was an identity to find. Quitting the search means we can create an identity that empowers us for living.

An empowered identity draws together all the resources we need for living, including the capacity to respond to crises. For example, by including the quality "I can learn to do just about anything," we cultivate the ability to take on new challenges with confidence. By choosing the thought "I'm adaptable," we establish the flexibility to respond to unexpected events.

Individual Process (20 minutes): In your journal, write

"My empowered identity." Record qualities you want in your identity that would increase your capability and flexibility for creating the kind of life you want.

Take a moment to identify a few life events that could overwhelm you. When you think of one, add a quality to your identity that would enhance your ability to cope with that situation.

What current challenges exist in your life or loom on the horizon? Note those.

Identify your most difficult challenge. Examining the qualities of your new identity, describe what resources you will bring to that challenge to successfully respond to it.

Recess of the mind: Take a few minutes to reflect on your discoveries.

If you are working with a partner or group, share your insights.

A feeling of freedom appears when you realize that there never was an identity to find, so you get to invent one. This removes the seriousness from the search for identity and adds creativity to life. When you learn to play with identity, it becomes more flexible. You can even have a bit of fun with the notion "I don't have the foggiest idea about who I am, but I'm willing to pretend." This playfulness encourages a more light-hearted approach to our lives.

Creating Meaning

What is the meaning of life? Is there a divinely ordained meaning? Are we just a bunch of animals flying through space on a rock? Do we create our own meaning?

Individual Process (15 minutes): On a journal page, note your first reactions to the question, "What is the meaning of life?"

Think of your answer as meaning that you created. Why did you make it up that way?

If we have been creating the meaning of our lives all along, we can become more playful about it. What establishes our meaning? The life purposes we create. Our purposes give our lives direction and help us decide what to do and what to avoid. By creating our purposes, we declare the goals we want our lives to serve.

Individual Process (25 minutes): Divide a journal page into quarters. In each part, create a life purpose. You may already be living in that purpose or you can create one you have not embraced yet. Your purpose might be to enhance the well-being of children, to cultivate cooperation, or to make an important scientific discovery. These are your purposes, so create what you want as goals for your life.

Focusing on your purposes, write your life mission. Your mission establishes the general meaning of your life as a choice.

Now that you are clearer about your life's purposes and mission, write a brief letter to yourself describing what you should be doing with your life. Be clear and direct.

If you are working with a partner or group, read your letters to each other. Describe new choices you have made or actions you will undertake given your new awareness.

> *When we are clear about our mission,*
> *we are clear about the meaning of our lives.*
> *Then, our lives have an objective and a direction.*
> *Through choice, we declare why we were born.*

Creating Ethical Principles

Our mission and life purposes establish direction, while ethical principles clarify how we will treat ourselves and others along the way. They add quality to the lives we create.

Woo Master:
"Wheel of harmony very simple.
Start by showing kindness.
Cannot show kindness? Try appreciation.
Cannot appreciate? Try respect.
Cannot respect? Try acceptance.
Cannot accept? Try kindness again.
Keep trying until wheel makes lovely sound."

Individual Process (20 minutes): In your journal, record ethical principles that help clarify how you want to treat yourself and others. Add a few that exist outside your normal way of thinking.

Explore what you have written. Remembering your life purposes, circle the principles that seem especially important to you.

From among them, select four to be your guiding principles.

On a new page, integrate your four life purposes and four ethical principles into a simple design. Then, contemplate your work as an image of the life you are going to create.

If you are working with a partner or group, share that life.

When we are clear about our life purposes and ethical principles, our lives take on a definite form, like distinctive works of art. Knowing there will never be another person like us, we cultivate our lives in harmony with our purposes and principles, so, when we leave, the garden we tended remains behind as a little reminder that we were here and made a small difference.

Woo Master:
"Life gardening is good reason to live.
With care, blossoms come."

Bibliography

Dreher, Diane. *The Tao of Inner Peace.* New York: HarperCollins Publishers, 1990.

Edinger, Edward. *The Creation of Consciousness.* Toronto: Inner City Books, 1984.

Elllison, Ralph. *Invisible Man.* New York: Random House, 1952.

Hoff, Benjamin. *The Tao of Pooh.* New York: Penguin Books, 1983.

Jacobi, Jolande. *The Way of Individuation.* New York: New American Library, 1967.

Jung, Carl G. *Modern Man in Search of a Soul.* New York: Harcourt, Brace, and World, 1933.

Keirsey, David and Marilyn Bates. *Please Understand Me: Character and Temperament Types.* Del Mar, CA: Prometheus Nemesis Book Company, 1984.

Keirsey, David. *Please Understand Me II: Temperament, Character, Intelligence.* Del Mar, CA: Prometheus Nemesis Book Company, 1998.

Lao Tzu. *The Way of Life.* New York: Capricorn Books, 1962.

Rajneesh, Bhagwan Shree. *Journey Toward the Heart: Discourses on the Sufi Way.* San Francisco: Harper and Row, 1976.

Sanford, John. *Healing and Wholeness.* New York: Paulist Press, 1977.

Stein, Murray. *Map of the Soul.* Chicago and La Salle, Il: Open Court Press, 1998.

Stevens, Anthony. *Jung.* Oxford: Oxford University Press, 1994.

Storm, Hyemeyohsts. *Seven Arrows.* New York: Harper and Row, 1972.

Walker, Brian. *Hua Hu Ching: The Unknown Teachings of Lao Tzu.* New York: HarperCollins Publishers, 1992.

Woodman, Marion. *Addiction to Perfection:The Still Unravished Bride.* Toronto: Inner City Books, 1982.

Heifer International

Heifer International is a nonprofit world hunger charity that gives income-producing cows, goats, sheep, water buffalo, rabbits, chickens, geese, ducks, bees, and other farm animals to needy, malnourished families in 46 countries around the globe. Its programs lift people from poverty while they encourage more community development, education, sound agricultural practices, gender equity, and spirituality. Recipients "pass on the gift" of offspring of their livestock to others in need, thus avoiding the stigma of accepting charity by becoming Heifer donors and partners. Heifer has changed the lives of 4 million families in 120 countries since its inception in 1944. It is not a disaster relief agency, but rather an effort to help the world's 700 million people who are chronically malnourished. It is funded by religious groups of many denominations, by private donations and by grants, and it has received widespread praise, including recognition from former presidents Carter, Reagan, Bush and Clinton. Donors' lives, too, are transformed when they discover that their tax-deductible contributions can have a real impact on global problems that sometimes seem hopeless. Heifer has farms that serve as education centers on world hunger in Perryville, Ark., Ceres, Calif., and Overbrook Farm in Rutland, Mass., and conducts world study tours so donors can see the positive impact Heifer is having around the world. Heifer means it when it says it is "saving the world one family at a time." To learn more about the good work and projects of Heifer International, visit its website: [www.heifer.org].

About the Author

Jim Downton has taught at the college level for thirty-six years. Currently, he is a Professor of Sociology at the University of Colorado, Boulder. Teaching is one of his deepest commitments. He teaches undergraduate courses in human development and creativity and frequently offers workshops on creative teaching for graduate students and faculty. His commitment to innovative teaching has earned him the University's two teaching excellence awards. He is also deeply involved in the International and National Voluntary Service Training Program (INVST) at the University of Colorado, an innovative leadership training program for upper division students that emphasizes civic responsibility and community service. To learn more about INVST, visit its website: [www.colorado.edu/ArtsSciences/INVST].

In the community, Jim offers workshops in human development and creativity. In addition to teaching and writing, he enjoys painting and sculpture. His life revolves around the issues of wholeness and creativity, which are ways of cultivating inner peace, happiness, and an easier way of living.

Printed in the United States
1275200004B/346-363